Introduction......

I think I should say straightaway that if you're a girl reading this Introduction you've probably got the book the wrong way round. I'll give you a second to check. That is to say, check whether you've got the book the wrong way round. Or check whether you're a girl or not. If you can't remember, that is. Done it? Good. I shall now assume that I am addressing myself exclusively to chaps, males, blokes, lads, boyos, etc. And possibly a few "don't-knows".

I say this because this section of the book is specifically aimed at us lads. After all, coping with girls is hard enough without them finding out how we do it! That would give them an unfair advantage and personally I think they've got that already. Yes, I know, I know, we're always being told that it's a "Man's World", but I believe that's just propaganda put out in a desperate attempt to make us poor hard-done-by fellas feel better. It was probably dreamed up by a woman. It's just the sort of thing they would do.

3

I mean to say, just think about it for a second. Think back to when you were very small. Just a baby, in fact.[1] Who was it used to tell you what to do? Your mum. A woman, probably. And, as I am pretty sure you all realize, a woman is just a girl in a Marks and Spencer's cardigan. So, you see, from the word go (or in the case of most babies, "goo"), it was a female who told you what to do. And it doesn't stop there. Oh, no! When you started school, who was it told you to get up? Mum! That woman again! When you were doing something perfectly harmless to your pet gerbil, who was it told you to stop getting blood on the carpet? Mum. That woman again!

OK, so Dad shouts occasionally, but you can tell he doesn't really mean it. He's only doing it to assert himself, make everyone realize that he's still there, and that he's not just a newpaper with a pair of old trousers pinned to the bottom. After all, it's not his fault that he

1. If you're still just a baby and are reading this, then I hope your parents realize you're advanced for your age!

gets all those official-looking letters that seem to assume he's the Head of the Household. He knows, just as well as everyone does, that he isn't. A dad is a bit like the Queen,[1] in that he's the sort of Constitutional Head of the Family, just as she is of the Nation (and, let's face it, you need a strong constitution to be the Head of most families!). But, just like the Queen, a dad doesn't actually make any of the important decisions that affect the running of the home. Like "What are we going to have for tea?" (i.e. Are we going to have Mr Wimby's Individual Steak-Extract Pies, followed by projectile vomiting, or tinned spaghetti on toast followed by sitting quietly for several hours while your stomach tries to identify it and decide what to do with it.)

Who decides what you wear? Not your dad, certainly. In fact, most dads don't even decide what they're going to wear themselves. This is partly because a dad gets most of his clothes as Christmas presents, but mainly because he only gets the privilege of buying himself a new shirt or trousers when Mum has got sick of looking at him in the old ones. In fact, dads usually let mums choose which shirt/trousers to buy. Because dads usually realize that they are firmly locked in mortal combat.

1. Actually, my dad is very like the Queen. Same colour wellies and everything. Although he doesn't have four thousand lunatic corgis snapping at his heels!

The Battle of the Sexes. A battle they have little or no hope of winning. In fact, it's more than a battle – it's a war. But because it has never been officially declared, it's more of a Cold War. Which, on winter nights, can develop into a hot-water bottle war. And that is what this book is about: The Battle of the Sexes. And although it may be impossible for us to win, chaps, I hope that with the aid of this book you might be able to come second equal. So read, learn and inwardly digest. But don't, whatever you do, reveal the secrets contained between these pages to a GIRL! For they are, at least for the purposes of this book, the ENEMY!

Coping with being a Boy

Before we can even attempt to understand (and thus cope with) the workings of the female mind, we must understand what makes boys tick. Of course, I'm not suggesting that boys tick in the literal sense of the word. I mean, boys don't, in reality, tick[1] any more than girls do, in fact. But what boys do do, and girls usually don't, is get dirty. And here we are not talking "smut" (see *vulgarity*, page 67). My understanding is that girls can get every bit as smutty as boys. No. We are talking good honest mud. They say that mud sticks, and in the case of your average boy, it does. Very easily. Why should this be? I'll tell you. Boys get Stuck In. In fact, boys get stuck in everything: glue, paint, and knot-holes in fences specifically constructed to stop people seeing what is going on behind them. Anything and everything. Including mud. And why? Because boys are natural

---

1. Although I was at school with one lad who did tick. We all just assumed that it was something he'd eaten. It turned out that we were right. He'd swallowed a novelty alarm clock, in the shape of Bertie Bassett. He was a short-sighted boy with a very big mouth. The doctors were not unduly worried. After all, time passes, doesn't it? Not in this case it didn't. The poor fella – Colin his name was – was excused all forms of competitive sport, because his alarm always went off at the wrong moment, giving him an unfair advantage (not to mention a terrible shock!). So he sat on the touchline alone, apart from the other twenty of us whose forged notes explained that we were all suffering from terminal verrucas. There we sat, with time on our hands. Well, all of us apart from Colin. He had time lodged somewhere near his pancreas.

explorers. They have an in-built thirst that sends them questing for knowledge. Girls, on the other hand, are just nosey.

Coping with parents

It's not easy being a boy. Being a boy is tough because, even from a very early age, a great deal is expected of you. Dads want you to play for your national football team, and they don't give up, do they? Oh, no. And if you're the firstborn, it's even worse. You get the old Son and Heir bit. They expect you to grow up and discover a cure for cancer while heading in a particularly tricky pass from Paul Gascoigne in a last-minute bid to clinch the match against Argentina in the World Cup which this year is taking place at the summit of a polar ice-cap for some strange reason. Merciful Heavens! Do those stupid parents of yours realize just how much skill and dexterity goes into getting your forehead to an ice-covered match ball when you're dressed in full arctic gear?

And what do these same devoted but ambitious parents expect of your sister? Nothing as long as she marries a nice bloke. Preferably one called Keith, who is either (a) capable of discovering a cure for cancer while heading in a particularly tricky pass from Paul Gascoigne in a last-minute etc., etc., or (b) a double-glazing salesman.

It's just not fair, is it? But then, there's nothing in the rules of life that says anything about it being fair. And

Lord knows I've looked often enough! You'll just have to grin and bear it. Preferably a stupid inane grin that will convince your parents you're irretrievably insane and should be left well alone.

Coping with other boys

But as if pressure from parents isn't bad enough, we poor blokes have to put up with an awful lot of pressure from other blokes, don't we? And it doesn't get any easier, I can tell you. At least not until you're about a hundred and four, and you know for a fact that neither you nor any of the other blokes in the "Bideawee Home for the Notentirelyallthere" are physically capable of any of the things you're all boasting about.

That's the big problem with boys (other boys, anyway), isn't it? They do like to boast. About anything. It's probably the only fault that blokes have, really. And it's probably our mothers' fault. I expect that if we had a medical expert sitting with us right now (you while you're reading this book and me while I'm writing it), this medical expert would tell you that boasting can be traced back to the wrong baby food. Or cow's milk. Anyway, something you definitely had no control over. But what can you do about it? Nothing, that's what! That part of your personality has been formed before you can even talk, let alone say "for goodness' sake, Mother, don't give me cow's milk. It'll make me boastful in later life."[1] Still, you can't really blame your mum, can you? She's only a woman, after all!

But how does this boasting manifest itself? It can't only be things like:

"I bet my handwriting's worse than your hand-writing."

"Bet it's not."

"Well, I can't even do joined-up, so there!"[2]

It may be interesting to note at this point that although girls do boast a bit, they are not nearly as good at it as boys, and rarely if ever do they boast about their handwriting. This is because girls' handwriting is generally very good, and is therefore not worth boasting about. This partly explains why there are so few women doctors.)

Boys generally boast about their prowess at sport (or their skill at avoiding it). This is not something they do for pleasure, but more because they are pressured into it by Parental and Tutorial Expectation. Or, to put it another way, in proper English, it's Mum's, Dad's and Teacher's fault. Let's face it, what are you supposed to do if you're continually being told that Neil Chapman is better at football than you are? Do you say:

"Yes. I noticed that."

1. I say later life, but in fact the incidence of cows-milk-induced boasting statistically can occur as early as the age of seven. According to Sir Arthur Peastring, Historian, Expert on Ancient China and All-Round Bighead, the youngest recorded boaster was P'u Yi, a five-year-old member of the Manchu Dynasty. But then, he was the Emperor of China, so I suppose he had something to shoot his mouth off about, really!

2. This particular snippet of boyish banter was recorded in 1937 by W. G. Artichoke, a child psychologist and all-in wrestler. I am reliably informed that the two boys taking part, who were 17 at the time, are now leading members of Her Majesty's Government.

Don't be silly! Are you a man or a mouse?[1] You try to get better at football. You struggle against all odds and a total lack of co-ordination and ball-control, until either (a) you become better at football than Neil Chapman, or (b) everyone in the class who is better at football than you are is struck by lightning in a freak sporting accident, leaving you the best player in the school. (And, incidentally, leaving your school without a cat in hell's[2] chance of ever carrying off the Fardby and Simcox Inter-Schools Junior League Challenge Cup.)

HERE NEIL, HOLD THIS LIGHTNING ROD

So why would any self-respecting lad want to put the reputation of his school (not to say his school's football team) at risk, simply to be better than one of his classmates? The answer is – he wouldn't. But would he bend over backwards, forwards and every other way simply to satisfy the ambitions of his parents, then? No. Not really. So what is the real reason behind these boyish excesses? Well, I'm afraid to say that the answer is one of the cruellest twists of fate imaginable. The answer is that, although this self-respecting lad does not realize it at the time, and indeed may never realize, he is probably doing it to impress a GIRL.

1. Extensive research has not revealed any incidences of mice being any good at football at all, which certainly must prove something.
2. Although there is no evidence to suggest that cats have ever played football either in Hell or out of it they are quite nifty with a ball of wool.

Now I can hear some of you saying: "That's ridiculous! I don't even *like* girls!" But that's one of the great and mysterious wonders of life.

It's also one of the things that sets us apart from other animals. The basic form seems to be that tiny children are more or less oblivious to the opposite sex, other than seeing them as someone who might want to pinch their squeaky Postman Pat, bottom or rusk. It seems to be that when young Jimmy starts playschool, he suddenly starts coming home and announcing that he's going to marry Melanie Coalbucket. She's the cute blonde one with the bunches (why do three-year-old kids always go for blondes?). That's Tuesday. By Wednesday Melanie is history. You have to cancel the church and send back the presents and everything. Jimmy is now swapping *sticklebricks*[1] with Carla Fenchurch. Obviously it's not serious! They're only three, after all! It *is* a bit worrying when Carla's dad wants to know what little Jimmy's

WAIT TILL HE'S OUT OF STICKLEBRICKS, THEN CHARGE

1. I'm referring here to the construction toy, not the fish. As you know, it's totally impossible to confuse the one with the other. *Sticklebricks* are short and thin with spikes all along the side, whereas *sticklebacks* are ... er ... short and thin with spikes all along the side. As you see ... totally different!

prospects are. All you can tell him is that Jimmy has his heart set on being a Fireman-Crocodile–Hunter, a notoriously precarious profession.

Then, all of a sudden, Jimmy starts Infant School, and within six months, women are out of the window. Yuck! Smelly! Horrible! Why? How does this happen? Is it Nature's way of getting us to settle down to studying without distractions? I think this is very unlikely. Because if this were the case, why would Nature wait until you were right in the middle of a really important school project, test or exam, with not a cat in hell's chance of passing unless you work flat out night and day . . . why would Nature choose this very moment to make you fall head over heels in love with Pamela Bostick, a girl you've never really spoken to, let alone liked! A girl that you have certainly never been stuck on!

Why does this happen? How does it happen? What twist of fate is it that governs the fact that you can totally hate girls one moment, then suddenly feel as though you can't live without them the next? Well, it's just one of the great mysteries of life that have foxed greater brains than mine for centuries. It is also, however, a strange quirk of human nature that we have to learn to live with, and cope with. And that is where this book can certainly help.

To assess something as complex and confusing as this, we really need to dig back into the past, to try to see if there is a key to this strange relationship between male and female, which has been characterized as The Battle of the Sexes. Whether, in fact things have always been this way, or whether there was a starting point, a moment when the war was declared and battle lines were drawn. So, let's have a quick dig back through history . . . .

Coping through history[1]

I blame God. Well, no. Let me rephrase that. I don't blame God. That's not the sort of thing you can do and hope to get away with it.[2] I respectfully suggest that God, if asked, would probably say, "This one's down to me, guys." After all, He created Man in His own image and called him Adam, a name that never really caught on. He then took a rib from Adam while he was sleeping and created woman, calling her Eve. (Where *did* he get those names from?)

He had to do it while Adam slept for two reasons: (1) If Adam had been awake, it would have hurt, a lot. They didn't have local anaesthetic in those days. And (2) If Adam had been awake God would have had to ask him if he minded. After all, you can't go around whipping people's ribs out without asking, not even on the National Health. Not even if you're God. What's more, if God had asked, Adam would have wanted to know what He wanted the rib for.

"I want to make you a wife."

---

1. Or not, really!
2. Note of caution: if you are thinking of blaming God, and hoping to get away with it, don't do it standing under a tree in the middle of a thunderstorm. This is one of the mysterious ways in which God moves, or rather makes the trees move.

What would Adam want a wife for? He knew nothing whatsoever about Love, Marriage and that sort of stuff. In fact he knew very little about anything, apart from snakes and apples. And all he knew about snakes and apples was that one was called Granny Smith and the other wasn't.

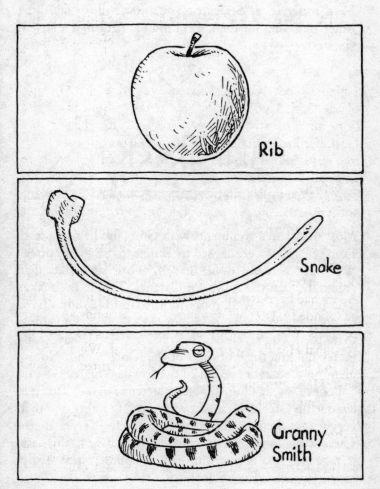

I have always found it hard to comprehend the concept of a woman being created from a rib. After all, it's rather trying to imagine "Bananarama" being descended from a box of takeaway barbecued bones. Impossible! Although, having heard them sing . . . Also, if God had asked Adam's opinion, surely Adam would have preferred a "Scalextric" or a football, or anything other than . . . but then, God didn't. And that's how it started.

Most of Adam's arguments with God (and he had a few, I can tell you!) were caused by things that Eve had done. Well, not actually done herself, more suggested that Adam did. Eat the apple, for instance. Talk to the snake. You might say "Well, more fool Adam! He didn't have to do it just 'cos Eve told him to!" Well, if you think that, then you're clearly a very very long way from understanding the workings of the female mind. Not to mention the staying power of the female tongue.

Believe me, it's quicker and quieter to agree! This is a lesson the Greeks learned pretty fast. It's also one that very few of them lived to regret, due to the *Trojan Wars*. These were fought over a woman. What else? In this case it was Helen of Troy, although it could just as easily have been Doris from Sainsbury's.

Ah! Helen of Troy. A great beauty, with "a face that launched a thousand ships",[1] at least in the opinion of the tabloid newspapers of the day. But love of her caused the Greeks to become devious beyond reason, and the Trojans to totally lose theirs (reason, that is). I refer, of course to the Wooden Horse of Troy.

1. I'm not sure exactly how she launched all these ships with her face. Maybe she banged her head on the side of the boat, instead of a bottle. That'd be just like a woman!

17

The Greeks laid siege to the city of Troy, but could not find a way of breaking into it. Then some bright Greek hit on the idea of building an enormous wooden horse, filling it with soldiers and leaving it outside the gates of Troy. The theory was that the Trojans would think it was a present, and take it inside the city. Completely stupid! Have you ever heard of a more ridiculous idea? Nor me! The amazing thing is, though – it worked! Yes! The Trojans went: "Oh, look! Some kind person has left us a lovely big wooden horse! Let's take it indoors and play with it!" Which they did, and barely had time to regret their decision before the Greek SAS had leapt out of the horse and nobbled the lot of them.

What were the Trojans thinking of, accepting presents in the middle of a war? I think something (or more likely someone) had addled their brains. And that someone was definitely Helen. The Trojans certainly learned never to underestimate the power of a woman's beauty. Not that many of them were around long enough to benefit from their newly-learned lesson.

I'VE GOT THE ANCIENT BLUES

Actually, the Romans have played more than a passing part in the Battle of the Sexes. Take Julius Caesar, for example. A warrior, a great leader, conquered half the known world and still found time to feed a few

Christians to the lions. Then what happens? He falls out with his best pal, Mark Anthony. And what caused this falling out? A matter of state? A matter of principle? No! A Girl? Yes! They both fell for the same girl. OK, admittedly she was the Queen of Egypt, and so beautiful that she'd make Miss World look like Nora Batty, but nevertheless! This is just one of the many cases throughout history of a really great friendship being broken up by a woman.

NO *I'M* GOING TO CLEOPATRA'S PARENTS' PLACE FOR THE CHRISTMAS BREAK!

When the Romans conquered Britain, most of the Brits just stood around covered in blue paint and let them get on with it. After all, they probably realized that we'd get our own back several centuries later by buying Italian time-share villas and littering their streets with lager cans and unconscious English football supporters. So naturally your average Briton was quite happy to let the Romans get on with building roads, improving the sewage system and renaming all the towns so that they ended in "-chester". But not so Queen Boadicea

19

(pronounced "Boo-Dicker").[1] So, just when everyone else is saying, "Don't rock the boat and the Romans will leave",[2] Boadicea was saying, "Let us drive them from our land by force!" (i.e. fight them). What's more, she didn't intend to do things by halves. Oh, no! She fitted her chariot wheels with huge blades which had a serious halving effect on the Roman soldiers' legs. Boadicea

COULD YOU SET THEM AT HALF LEG PLEASE?

1. That's another difference between the sexes. Their names. Women have names that are spelt very differently from the way they're pronounced, such as Siobhan ("Sher-Vorn"), while boys have names like Bob ("Bob").
2. Which of course eventually they did, proving who was right. Namely the blokes.

intended these blades to frighten the Romans and make them run away, but how could they run away with their legs cut in half? This is one of the earliest examples of that phenomenon now known as "Feminine Logic".

And what was the net result of Boadicea meddling in matters that didn't concern her and that she clearly didn't understand? Total chaos! Chaos that we still have to cope with today. Roads, for instance. If the Romans had been left to get on with improving our roads, we would never have had to put up with the M25. The British have never been any good at roads. It's just not the sort of thing we're good at. We excel in other things, like . . . er . . . not roads, anyway. So, next time you're stuck on a motorway and steam is pouring out of the car radiator and your father's ears and your mum is sitting there with the map the wrong way up saying "I'm sure we should have turned off at Chipping Norton", you'll know who to blame. Boadicea. A woman. But it doesn't end there . . ..

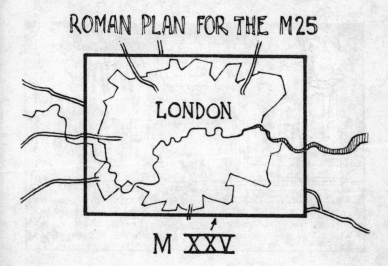

ROMAN PLAN FOR THE M25

LONDON

M XXV

There is a popular (popular among girls, anyway!) belief that the knights who went to the Holy Land to fight alongside Richard the Lionheart enjoyed themselves. In fact, if you're fool enough to read the other (girlie) half of this book, you might almost get the impression that they wanted to go! Isn't that silly? I mean, think about it! Which would you rather do? Go off to the Middle East to run around all day in a suit of armour under the boiling hot desert sun, or join Robin Hood's band? No contest, right? But women can't see that! So why did they go? I'll tell you. They were badgered into it. Yes. By their womenfolk.

You can just imagine it, can't you? Living in a big draughty castle with no electricity or anything, forever having to fight the neighbours because they wanted to hunt your deer, pillage your village, or park their boat in your moat. Nothing going on from one end of the year to the next. Well, nothing worth making a tapestry about, anyway. The womenfolk forever moaning about the lack of double-glazing, or the fact that you haven't got around to putting any shelves up yet (doesn't she realize that the hammer and power drill haven't been invented yet?). So, when a messenger comes round saying that the king is putting together a bunch of likely lads for a trip abroad, and there could be a knighthood in it, you have to go, don't you? Stands to reason! Especially when the alternative is sitting around at home getting an earbashing!

It was also a question of chivalry. Something that women in those days held very dear. They got very cross if you didn't open the drawbridge for them, or give up your seat on the last horse and cart home from the pictures. Why, some of them even expected you to be prepared to *die* for them! Particularly in . . .

23

Where the knights fought, and killed each other, in order to win the favour of a lady. And what did this favour consist of? The right to tie her hanky on the end of your lance. And you could never be sure that it was a clean one! Ah, Camelot! Yet another example of a close friendship being broken up by a woman. Poor King Arthur, for instance. Yes, I know that he probably never existed, but that doesn't alter the fact that if Lancelot hadn't fallen for Guinevere, Camelot might still be standing today, even if it was a myth. Then of course there was . . .

HENRY VIII

Poor Henry! He had to get married six times in order to get a male heir. In fact, he even had to invent the Church of England, so that he could get a divorce. Of course, divorce was a complicated business in those days.[1] So Henry, being a practical sort of bloke, took to chopping

1. Actually divorce these days isn't the least bit complicated. You can now get married and divorced in the same day, and still have time to go to Macdonald's.

24

his wives' heads off instead. Of course, what he never realized was that it is the male who determines the sex of a child. His doctors knew this, of course, but they weren't going to tell him, were they? I mean, you don't need a brain the size of the Basildon Arndale Centre to realize that telling the King of England he's going about things the wrong way is not exactly the wisest move of all time!

25

QUEEN ELIZABETH

She was the first really serious Queen of England. By which I mean that she was the first really significant Queen. There were tremendous advances throughout the first Elizabethan era, as it has become known. The potato was discovered. Tobacco. In fact various things that are really dangerous for your health.

Beheading. Elizabeth did a fair amount of that. She

GOVERNMENT WARNING BEHEADING CAN SERIOUSLY DAMAGE YOUR HEALTH

even chopped the head off one of her own family, Mary, Queen of Scots. A distant relative, she lived in Scotland. At least she did until Elizabeth invited her to England for a short back and sides! And why? Just to show her who was boss, really! Oh, yes! They said at the time that

Mary was plotting against Elizabeth, which is very likely as they were both girls, but isn't it just typical, eh? Give a girl a whole kingdom to play with, and what does she do? Fall out with her family! Mind you, she didn't do the head-chopping herself, even though it might have been fun. She got a man to do it. Very devious, eh? Getting a man to do the dirty work. Still, I suppose if you're Queen you can get away with that sort of thing.

Whatever else she may or may not have done, Elizabeth didn't do an awful lot for equality. It wasn't exactly her fault. Half the population thought she was a man in a frock, so what could she do? In fact, it wasn't really until the reign of Queen Victoria that women really had a voice, and even then, not much of one.

QUEEN VICTORIA

Most of the advances in the Victorian era were due to her husband, Albert. He was a great supporter of Crystal Palace and never missed a match. He also had a great sense of humour. So much so that when he died, Victoria banned the telling of jokes, mainly because she wasn't any good at it. No matter what funny story she was told, she just said: "We are not amused." It was a very miserable time, and everyone went around in black. Even women got a bit fed up with this, though they'd learned to put up with more or less anything over the years. So, at the turn of the 20th century the Suffragettes started campaigning for the vote.

THE SUFFRAGETTES

They chained themselves to railings, threw themselves under horses and generally got in everyone's way. Still, it got them out of the house. And what's more, it got women the vote. And it's been downhill more or less from there on in, really.

It probably seems very strange now that there was a time, not very long ago, when women didn't have the right to vote. But they didn't. They were kept very firmly "in their place", wherever that is. In some cultures they still are. No woman is allowed to step into a Sumo wrestling ring, for example. I can't imagine any woman being particularly bothered about that. Unless of course she was the size of a house and looking for a job. But I suppose a woman would consider it a matter of principle: why should she be denied the right to do something that she doesn't want to do anyway because it's totally unsuitable for her? (That good old female logic again!).

Why have men throughout history denied women the same basic rights that they have themselves, if indeed they have? Well, I would have thought it was obvious. Women take over. I mean, let a girl in your gang, and before you know where you are she's organizing things, making you keep the gang-hut tidy, suggesting colour schemes and so on. But we blokes like things rough and ready, don't we? At least, we do until a female comes along and offers to make everything cosy and comfy. But the trouble is, just when we're sitting there congratulating ourselves on finding a slave, we realize that we're doing all the running round, and she's doing all the organizing. Look at Margaret Thatcher.[1]

MARGARET THATCHER

She was the first Prime Minister to be called Mrs. All the others were called by their full name, weren't they? Edward Heath, Harold Wilson, William Pitt the Elder, William Pitt the younger, William Pitt the Older Than he Looks, Benjamin Disraeli, John Major . . . The point is that none of them were called "Mrs", were they? Not

1. Oh, go on! Just a quick squint!

even behind their backs. But she was! Oh, yes! She was treated with respect, fear almost. I bet even the Cabinet never called her Margaret. Not even Douglas Hurd.

"Have you written that new European policy document, Douglas?"

"Yes, Mrs Thatcher. And I've put up those shelves in the welly cupboard like you told me to."

Cor! I bet she gave them the runaround! I bet they had to wipe their feet before they went into Number Ten wash their hands before dinner!

But women are like that. They act the innocent, we let them into our domains, and within minutes they've totally reorganized the system and got everyone doing their own washing-up! And to make matters worse, they

often prove to be better at things than their male counterparts! It's not fair! I mean, it's bad enough being a bloke and having to compete against other blokes . . . but when you have to start competing against girls as well . . .

So who are these people so often referred to as the fairer sex? It's time to examine them in some detail! Pass the surgical gloves!

What is a girl?...

"Sugar and spice and all things nice. That's what little girls are made of." Whoever wrote that has never bitten one.

But what are they? Are they human? Where do they come from? How soon can they be sent back there?

To answer these questions, and the entire mystery surrounding the female animal, we need to start at the bottom. Sorry, not the bottom. I mean with the basics. Not quite the same thing at all!

How to spot one

Look around you. Actually, if you're completely alone, don't bother. But if you're in the classroom, or any mixed-sex environment, look around you. Look past the kid with the pencil up his nose. Look past the kid who appears to be removing his brain via his earhole. Do you see the kids who look different? The ones with skirts, I'm talking about, not the ones with the extra head who have just arrived at your school from another galaxy (nice kids, messy eaters). Concentrate on the ones in skirts. The ones in skirts are GIRLS.[1] Congratulations! You have spotted the major difference (in appearance, anyway) between boys and girls. Skirts. There are other physical differences, obviously, but this is not the time or the place to start discussing all that. If you can tell the

1. If the skirts are tartan, then the ones in skirts are probably the Massed Pipes and Drums of the Argyll and Sutherland Highlanders.

31

difference between trousers and skirts, then you can tell boys from girls. Unless they're wearing jeans.[1]

Let us assume that you've managed to sort the girls from the boys, in your own mind at least. And talking of minds, this is the precise area where the male and female of the human animal vary totally. This is unusual. In most species the difference is purely physical. The male peacock for example, is resplendent and stunningly handsome, the female drab and boring. Not so different from humans really. But the brains of the male and female peacock are identical.[2] Not so the human male

BRAIN

and female. The male human brain is logical, concise and clear-thinking. The female human brain is a mystery that has baffled scientists for centuries. The popular theory is that it was created by an over-enthusiastic Archangel Subcommittee on God's afternoon off.[3] God probably said: "Here, you lot are always shooting your mouths off, telling me where I'm going wrong. Here's a rib, see what you can do with that. I'm going to Sainsbury's."[4]

1. Is this why most schools don't allow girls to wear jeans to school? I expect so.
2. They are both mind-wrenchingly stupid.
3. It is interesting to note that in countries that still practise cannibalism, the male human brain is a rare delicacy, whereas the female human brain sells for about fourpence a tonne.
4. Actually it's slightly more likely that God said: "I'm going to *create* Sainsbury's."

So Man was created in God's image, but Woman was created by committee. It makes sense. When you see what committee involvement has done to Basingstoke, it goes some of the way to explaining why women, whether young or old, are as they are. But does it make them any easier to cope with? Of course it doesn't!

Let's try a different approach: the approach of "divide and rule". By that I mean let's try and isolate some of the different types of girls/women/females, and see if that helps us cope any more easily with them. It probably won't, but it's worth a try!

For the purposes of this exercise I'll break the types down into headings, like this:

Type: Type of girl, obviously!

Nature and habitat: That's basically what they're like and where you're likely to find them.

What they say: Some typical remark that the type might make.

What they mean: Bound to be something completely different from what they say!

Pros and cons: The particular type's good points and bad points. Maybe this section should just be *Cons*!

WHAT A CHEEK!

Types of girls...

1: The Tomboy

Nature and habitat: Any lad who ever had a gang has met the tomboy. There's one in every gang. It's a measure of just how fearless this type is that they join a boys' gang at the time when all the members of that gang are sworn girl-haters. It's also a measure of the ugliness of this type that no-one actually realizes that she *is* a girl. By the time they do realize, she's so much "one of the boys" that she's more or less accepted.

What they say: Oddly (though typically!), the tomboy is not above using her sex to get her own way. So a typical remark might be: "Oi! There's a lady present!" Although of course she no more regards herself as a lady than any of the rest of the gang do.

What they mean: "Pack that in, or I'll thump yer!"

Pros and cons: The good thing about having a tomboy in your gang is that when you go off torturing baby frogs and on to torturing girls, you've got one to practise on. The bad thing is that if you should try anything, she'll make you wish you'd stuck to torturing frogs!

2: The Raving Beauty

Nature and habitat: She is in every song ever written. She is also in the most inaccessible corner of the classroom. She is the subject of fantasies, fictions, boasts and brawls. And throughout it all, she remains aloof.

What they say: "Hi!"

What they mean: "Don't even bother to think about it, sonny!"

Pros and cons: She is a delight to look at. Unfortunately looking is not enough. Also unfortunately she surrounds herself with a posse of ex-tomboys that make the cast of "Prisoner, Cell Block H" look like a Miss World contest.

3: The Personal Organizer

Nature and habitat: To be found in virtually every after-school society there is. And when she's not there, she can be found about two paces behind you! For you have been selected as her mission. She intends to organize you. What has happened is that her mothering instinct has blossomed well ahead of her sex drive. So she doesn't actually fancy you. Not yet!

What they say: "Have you done your homework?"

What they mean: It would be nice to think that she meant "'Cos if you have, can I copy it?", but she doesn't. She actually means exactly what she says!

Pros and cons: Although it's quite nice to have your own walking Filofax, the problem is that the diary might suddenly decide that it fancies you! Then you're for it!

4: The Groupie

Nature and habitat: You'll find her on the touchline at every school sporting event, seemingly the team's biggest fan. But listen carefully to her cheers. Don't they sound more like jeers?

What they say: "Come on our side!" (very loudly).

What they mean: "Our dog could do better than you lot!"

Pros and cons: Yes, it's very nice to have someone on the touchline. Let's face it, the rest of the school don't even seem to realize that there *is* a football team. But the trouble with the groupie is that she has this ability to reduce grown blokes to quivering masses of insecurity with a curl of her lip. You can only hope that one day she'll stop turning up to matches because she's found herself a boyfriend. The problem is going to be finding someone brave or foolish enough to take her on.

5: The Know-All

Nature and habitat: To be found at the top of the class, at the front of the race, on the platform of the school debating society. In fact, anywhere where there's a chance to be first. That's where she is. For she's that rare thing, a Very Intelligent Female. And, boy, doesn't she know it!

What they say: "Gosh! Don't you know?"

What they mean: "How can anyone be as thick as you and survive?"

Pros and cons: A great friend to have because you can always crib her work. However, a friendship would not be on the cards because a five-minute conversation with her would leave you gasping!

6: The Go-Between

Nature and habitat: Every class has one. And if you suddenly find that you have a passion for a girl in your class, but don't know how to tell her, this is the girl to go to. Come wind, hail or driving blizzard, she will get the message through!

What they say: "Leave it to me – I'll tell her!"

What they mean: "I'll do even better than that!"

Pros and cons: And there's the rub, because although she will get the message through quicker than the *News of the World*, her similarity to that Sunday newspaper does not end there. She will tell your dream girl of your undying love, then enlarge on it, embroider it, add a few frills and tell everyone else!

7: The Spy

Nature and habitat: To be found wherever they shouldn't be when you least want them there. If they are also your little sister, this makes them doubly deadly. Little brothers also fall into this category, but girls are better at it!

What they say: Nothing. They don't need to. The sniggering has the desired effect!

What they mean: They mean to cause as much trouble as they possibly can. In some situations, you might almost suspect that they are in the pay of your parents. You would probably be right!

Pros and cons: Well, of course, this kind of irritation could be put to good use. It could, for instance, be used to frighten off an unwanted girlfriend. But if you're thinking this, think again! The spy is not on your side, and can't be bought. Not by you, anyway!

8: The Limpet

Nature and habitat: Not to be confused with the personal organizer. These ones don't want to organize you. They will love you to the grave, however muddly you are. They appear to be magnetically attached to you. Even if you are in separate rooms, houses or towns (or planets even), you can feel them looking longingly at you. Hear them sigh every time you move your elbow.

What they say: It sounds like; "Huuuuuuuuuhhhhhh." Someone with no soul would call it a sigh. They wouldn't even be close.

What they mean: The words have not been invented to describe it. Even if Wordsworth, Robert Browning and Keats were to stay up all night using one of those computerized poetry machines, they couldn't even scratch the surface.

Pros and cons: True love is beautiful. Unfortunately, the limpet isn't!

Well . . . those are a few of the examples of types of girls that you can expect to bump into as you slide along the razor-blade of life. There are many more. Many, many more. Too numerous to list here. In fact, if we were to attempt it, this book would not be available in a handy-sized paperback version, but only in forty-eight volumes via your front door from a seedy-looking ex-double-glazing salesman in a shiny suit.

So because the different types are more numerous than the hairs on a human head,[1] perhaps the solution to the problem of coping with girls lies in providing you with an easy reference of handy tips, hints and so forth. Right! That's what we'll do then! Prepare to be amazed by the . . .

1. And I'm not referring to Elton John's head, either!

The A to Z of coping with girls.....

You will notice that this section of the book deals largely with coping with girls once you have reached that unhappy state of being interested in them again, having gone all the way through middle school realizing that they are rubbish and best ignored. During this period the only females who blight your life are your mum (who's a parent and as such is probably only doing what she sees as her job) and your teachers (who are really the same as parents, with the addition of chalk-dust and sensible shoes). It is therefore hardly surprising that when the moment comes for your hormones, the devil at your elbow or whoever it is, to tell you that it's time to like girls, you are hardly equipped to cope. That is what this A to Z is all about.

Possibly the easiest way of leading you gently through the minefield of coping with girls is to provide you with an easy-reference A to Z. Possibly this isn't the easiest way of doing it, but it's the way I'm going to do it anyway!

You will notice that I have made this easy-reference A to Z even easier to use by arranging it in alphabetical order. I have thought of everything! Actually it is possible that I *haven't* thought of everything, so you may have to fill in the gaps yourself, from your own experience. Good luck!

acne: (*ak-ney* noun)

It's a sad fact (but true) that there comes a time in every young man's life when his face breaks out in terrible spots. This happens to a lesser or greater extent. The lucky ones get away with one teeny-weeny blemish. The unlucky ones wind up looking like the dark side of the Moon! This is called acne. It's also called zits, spots, plukes, and a variety of other things too numerous (or too rude) to print here.

Now, acne would be much easier to cope with if it happened in that period of one's development that I have referred to elsewhere, when you don't even like girls. No such luck! Oh, no! Acne breaks out within twenty-four hours of you realizing that there's much more to life than football, conkers and leaving nasal deposits under your desk lid for consumption at a later date. You hate girls – you have skin like a baby's bottom. You fancy girls – suddenly you look like something out of *Terminator 2*. And there's nothing you can do about it. It's just one of those mysteries of life that you have to grin and bear. (But don't grin too hard in case your spots start to dribble). It's no consolation to learn that it happens to girls too. To a lesser degree usually, but then that's always the case, isn't it? The Good Lord dreams up something really "iffy", He always gives us poor guys a double dose, doesn't he?

So, what can you do? Wear a mask?

POPULAR ACNE TREATMENTS

brothers: (*bruth-erse* noun plur.)
Now, I bet you're saying to yourself: "Brothers? Hang on, I thought this was a book about coping with girls! What've brothers got to do with it?" Well, I'll tell you.

Imagine the situation: you are sitting on the sofa in the lounge, with the girl of your dreams. Well, the girl of this week's dreams, anyway. The lighting is low. You've managed to con her into thinking that the bulb blew just as you walked through the door. The romantic music goes on and on in the background (the CD's stuck). The moment is right. You can tell. It's time to make that all-important first move. Time to take her hand. That is, if you can get *your* hand from down the back of the sofa where you jammed it when you started to put your arm round her, then changed your mind. And, having retrieved it, will you be able to shake the cramp out of it without her thinking you're trying to karate her to death? (I bet this never happens to Richard Gere.)

Anyway, you're in this situation, but confident that you will overcome all obstacles and romance will blossom sometime between now and her last bus. It is at this very moment that you hear the tell-tale sound. Or smell the tell-tale smell. Yes! Your little brother is hiding behind the sofa. What is more, he has been there all the time. What is even more, he has heard everything you have said. All your best lines. The same best lines that he heard you telling the girl of last week's dreams. By now it is obvious to everyone that Little Brother is there. Obvious to everyone, that is, with normal hearing and a reasonable sense of smell. How many times have your parents told Little Brother not to eat the dog's food? It doesn't agree with the dog, so Heaven knows what it does to humans! (We'll call Little Brother a human for the sake of argument.)

So, what do you do? Normally a little creative torture is an ideal way of solving problems with siblings. But not in front of Her. You know for a fact that she hates the sight of blood.

So, how do you cope? The short answer is – you don't! You simply make a mental note to have the lounge swept by sniffer dogs next time you want to take a girl in there.

BEEP

I'M GETTING A READING ON MY BROTHER DETECTOR

Cool: (*kool* quality)
Oh yeah! You've seen them, haven't you? The blokes who think they're really cool. Not to mention the girls who think they're really cool. Not to mention the girls who think the blokes who think that they're really cool really *are* cool, or even the blokes who think that the girls who think they're really cool really are. Confused? You should be! Because there's really no such thing as "cool"! No! Honestly! It's a totally manufactured thing. Probably dreamed up by some media person who couldn't think of a word to describe something, so came out with "cool". A bit like "wicked", really.

But where does that leave us? Because, although "cool" as such doesn't exist, you try convincing someone who thinks you're *un*-cool that there's no such thing as that, either! It's a real problem. Made worse by the fact that everyone's idea of what "cool" means differs slightly. I mean, if you know that a particular girl likes really tall blokes and you're a shorthouse, then you know where you stand. You stand absolutely no chance of going out with her, right? But if she says: "I only like really cool blokes," how do you know what her definition of cool is? You can't ask her, can you? Oh, yes! Maybe you could try and draw up a mental picture of what she imagines is "cool" by saying stuff like: "I think The Beautiful South are really cool – what about you?", but by the time you've done the same with fashion, food, etc., etc., you'll probably have gone off her anyway. The best thing to do is be an individual. Who knows – the girls might regard that as being really cool. You can never tell with females.

dumping: (*dumb-ping* verb)
One of the least pleasant things about having any kind of relationship with the opposite sex is being "dumped". That is, being told in no uncertain terms that you are "not wanted on voyage", like a suitcase full of flares that spends life's journey shut in the attic. On the bright side, "dumping" can be a mixed blessing. You could be thinking of dumping the girl of this week's dreams, only to be told that you are yesterday's news as far as *she*'s concerned. You might think that in such a situation we would be able to be philosophical and say to ourselves: "Ah, well. At least I don't have to go through the whole business of dumping her now!" But we don't. Oh, no! We get all upset:

"Huh! How could she? Who does she think she is?"

Actually, she probably knows who she is. It's just that she's realized that you're not who she thought *you* were!

"That's the last time I buy her a bag of chips!" you whimper.

But let's assume for the moment that you know she has no intention of dumping you. Quite the reverse, in fact. She has every intention of spending the rest of her life with you, even though you're only twelve and have no prospects and even less chance of ever getting a single GCSE (even Metalwork). You know she feels this way by those tiny little tell-tale signs: she keeps walking really slowly past wallpaper shops, she's put your names down for the 200th series of "Mr and Mrs", and she's had your name tattooed across her face.

So, how do you let her down gently? Go missing and leave a pile of your clothes on a beach in Australia? Change your name to Lord Lucan? Start wearing a dress? What? Well, all these methods are possible, if a little complex and costly. The easiest way is to ask yourself what she would do, and do it first.

So, what would she do? Well, in these sorts of matters it has to be said that girls are better than boys at confronting the issue head-on. They understand that emotions change, that nothing is for ever and that there are times when showing a high level of maturity is called for. So, what would she do if she wanted to dump you? Easy! She'd get her mate to do it! (Take a look at *dates* in the other half of the book, just to get the whole picture. That is, of course, if you think you can believe any advice a woman gives you!)

disco: (*disk-o* noun)
Traditionally a great place to meet girls. Always assuming that you can get past the teacher-bouncer on the door ("by day he is mild-mannered Mr Fidgett the first-year master, by night he is Conan the Bouncing Barbarian!") and don't mind drinking school cola (the caretaker uses it to strip paint in the holidays). It's also a

great place to dance with girls, as long as you don't mind dancing with their five mates and their handbags. It is not, however, a great place to *talk* to girls, unless you have a voice like a foghorn and the hearing of an adult fruit bat. You'd stand a better chance of meeting a nice girl at the dentist. At least you'd know where her teeth had been!

WE ONLY CAME IN TO SWOP TELEPHONE NUMBERS

envy (*nv* noun)
Nothing can eat you up faster than envy. Except a Brontosaurus. But I wasn't really referring to that kind of eating up, and anyway Brontosauruses are extinct.

Envy can kill a relationship faster than getting dumped by your girlfriend's best friend, even if the best friend has had a lot of practice. You see, all sorts of relationships, from a simple friendship to true love (whatever that is), need working at. And you can't work at a friendship all the time you're envying someone else's friendship.

If you spend all your time going: "Cor! Look at Dave Plinkett! He's sitting next to Melanie Tideswell! Bet he's going out with her as well!" (Although experience will show you that sitting next to the girl of your dreams is often better than going out with her, because it's cheaper and you can do it more often.) If you are envying Dave,

49

chances are he's thinking that *you*'re the lucky one going out with Samantha Bikepump. He probably isn't, but he might be. Those glasses of his are very thick.

flirting (*fler-ting* verb)
Look up "flirting" in a dictionary and you'll discover that it means "wooing frivolously". It also means "to toy with". So, what I'm saying is that flirting should not be taken too seriously. You'll discover that flirting is something that girls enjoy, so you'll have to be able to tell the difference between flirting and serious attraction, otherwise it could end in tears. Yours probably. Not to mention the fact that the minute the rest of the girls in the class (school, world, universe as well, probably) get to hear that you misinterpreted a bit of totally harmless flirting for the Real Thing (whatever that is), you are going to be a laughing stock. Not to mention the other fact that the minute the rest of the boys in your class get to know that you "chatted up" Carol Leglock and she turned you down, well . . . I think you can guess the rest!

The great trick is to be able to tell the difference. So, how do you do it? Don't ask me! The problem is that the girls at school are only women with biro stains. And women reserve the *exclusive* right to change their minds. And because it *is* exclusive, you *boys* can't do it. Well, you can, but not if you want to live! So, if you suspect any girl of flirting with you, the best solution is probably to climb inside your desk, and get your best mate to nail the lid down. That way he can take the flak when she changes her mind. After all, what are mates for?

gifts (*giftz* noun plur.)
There comes a time in every young man's life when he feels the overwhelming urge to buy a female a present. It starts in childhood with a box of Newberry Fruits for your mum on her birthday. In fact, you never actually buy them yourself. You're just an accessory after the fact. But you're just as guilty in the eyes of the law. Buying your mum little gifts is seen as a Good Thing. Just as totally forgetting your dad's birthday is seen as completely normal. Even the type of gift is significant. For instance, for Christmas mums get perfume, flowers, beautiful things. Dads get socks. Socks! Huh! No man ever bought a woman a pair of socks. Unless they've got cold feet (the woman, I mean. If the man has got cold feet he usually buys the woman something very very expensive! Such is the nature of guilt!)

Of course, it is not realized at the time, but this gift-giving is being passed on from generation to generation, as part of the human culture. Hardly surprising, then, that when you find yourself, through no fault of your own, attracted to a girl, a little voice deep inside tells you to buy her a gift. Unfortunately, the little voice totally forgets to tell you *what* gift! And this is the problem.

I'VE ALREADY GOT ONE OF THOSE

The trick is to suit the gift to the situation. Here are some examples:

At the pictures Good gift: sweets or chocolates. But nothing crackly or sticky. There's nothing worse than not being able to hear the film for the rustle of paper, or hold her hand without getting covered in dribbly chocolate. And if you're buying chocolates, make sure that she isn't on a diet. Bad gift: a bunch of flowers. Where is she going to stick them all through the film?

At her house If you're invited round to her house (be very wary if you are. Things could be more serious than you realize), then the gift is very important. Good gift: a bunch of flowers, but check first that she doesn't suffer from hay fever! You don't want her sneezing and dribbling all over your best clobber, do you? But flowers are a great idea as they'll impress her parents. Also, her whole family can have a sniff, which saves you buying anything separate for them.

Bad gift: a magazine on wrestling. It could give her parents quite the wrong (or right!) idea about what the pair of you are going to get up to if you're left alone for five minutes!

At a restaurant! Good gift: a single rose. But leave the price tag on. This is so that the waiter won't think you've pinched it out of the vase on the table!

Bad gift: anything edible. This could spoil her appetite. Although if she's a big eater, then a medium sliced loaf could come in very handy and save you a fortune. Check her eating habits beforehand. You can do this by studying her desk in the classroom. Teethmarks in the lid or chunks missing from it are usually a bit of a giveaway!

At the disco Good gift: perfume. A little dab after a bit of dancing could prove very welcome. For you as well as the girl! But when I say perfume, I do mean perfume. We are not talking underarm deodorant here!

Bad gift: a bag of marbles. Not in itself a bad gift in the general scheme of things. It's certainly unusual, anyway. But it wouldn't be a good idea to give her marbles at a disco. She might drop them and cause a major pile-up.

A general note about gifts: don't expect to receive a gift in return. Girls tend not to give little gifts on dates. This is all part of the new equality.

A word of warning: they say that "diamonds are a girls' best friend." Find out if this is true of *your* particular girl as early on as possible, because frankly, the last thing you want is a girl with expensive tastes! (Sneak a look at "*No*" in the other half. If you must!)

SNEAK A LOOK AT THE OTHER HALF AND I'LL BIFF YOU ONE!

glasses (*glass-ez* noun)
Someone once said: "Men don't make passes at girls who wear glasses." But do girls make passes at men who wear glasses? Or do men who wear glasses make passes at girls who wear glasses? Or do girls who wear glasses make passes at men who wear glasses? Do men, for instance, who wear glasses make passes at girls who don't, and

vice versa? And what about contact lenses? Well, life is a mass of complications and glasses are no exception! But it does seem that the wearing of "specs" is no longer the barrier it once used to be to finding yourself attractive to girls. Modern specs are really very trendy – they might even be "cool", whatever that is!

SWOON
SWOON

humour (*hugh-mer* noun)

Men may not make passes at girls who etc., etc. but it is a known fact that girls respond to a sense of humour. Girls of all ages. Except very young girls, who would probably just think you were being stupid (if younger sisters are anything to go by). So let's forget them, if it's at all possible, and concentrate on older girls. Now, before you rush out and buy the *Bumper Book of the World's Funniest Jokes* (all of which are totally unfunny, by the way), it is not the telling of jokes that girls respond to. It is a sense of humour, which is a completely different thing. It is something you either have or haven't got. If you haven't got it, then I'm sorry but there's really nothing you can do about it. But if you're sitting there smugly thinking "I've got a great sense of humour all right! Oh, yes! Why, I only have to walk in the room and the girls are in stitches," then I would ask you to consider this carefully. Are they laughing with you, or *at* you?

Incidentally, never ask a girl to tell you a joke. They don't know any. (See what they've got to say about *Jokes*)

hate (*hate* noun)

Hate, they say, is very close to love. How does that song go: "She wore an Itsy Bitsy . . ." Oh, sorry! Wrong song! I've got it! It goes: "You always hurt the one you love." Oh, they don't write songs like that any more, thankfully. But it is true that love and hate are very close emotions. You only have to look at the front cover of Sharon Bingly's history exercise book to realize the truth of what I'm telling you. Have a look! Does it or does it not say: "Sharon loves/hates/loves/hates/loves/hates Jason Donovan"? Mind you, I think I know how she feels. The hate part anyway. But be careful. Just when you think that the girl of your dreams loves you to distraction, you could find that she hates you with just as much enthusiasm.

intelligence (*in-telly-gentz* noun)

If you want to impress a girl, for some reason best known to yourself, you could do a lot worse than be intelligent. Mind you, if you were that intelligent you'd probably realize that you were wasting your time. But let's assume that you are quite intelligent, but have a bit of a blind spot where girls are concerned. The answer is to not flash it about. Your intelligence, we're talking about.

Because nobody, not even a girl, likes a smarty-pants. They certainly don't like somebody who sounds smarter than they are. And I can understand. After all, nobody likes a know-all, do they?

But a little knowledge is a useful thing. It keeps the conversation going if you're on a date in, say, a restaurant, and you've been waiting for six hours for the main course (which is not unusual, unless you've ordered something hot. Then the wait can be anything up to several days). But choose your topic carefully. It can be something very simple, but given an interesting twist. The weather is not much of a topic. She has probably noticed that it's raining, especially if you're eating outdoors. So, the secret is: if you want to keep your girl, talk to her intelligently about subjects that you know interest her. But if you want to dump her (see *dumping*), switch straight away to train-spotting.

jealousy (*jelly-sea* noun)
Oh, dear! Jealousy has killed even more friendships than envy. Imagine the situation. You suddenly find that you are strangely attracted to this girl in your class/school/ youth club/branch of Trainspotters Anonymous/ whatever. Let's call her Mandy, shall we? You are strangely attracted to Mandy. I say strangely because not ten minutes earlier you thought you hated her. Now, amazingly, you would willingly die for her. Well, maybe "willingly" is an exaggeration, but you get the picture. Now. Just as suddenly you are consumed with jealousy about everyone who goes near her. You see everyone as a rival for Mandy's affections. And I mean everyone. Even your best mate, who is actively trying to persuade you not to make a fool of yourself by going out with her . . .

"Why is he doing that?" you think, irrationally. "I bet he wants her for himself!" you reason unreasonably. Even when a fly lands on her ear, you find yourself thinking: "What's that fly whispering to her?" Actually, flies are often landing on her ears, but you are too blinded by love to notice!

This is jealousy. And it is poisonous. Avoid it. Some blokes put their girlfriend on a pedestal, which certainly makes it very hard for short blokes to talk to her, but if you want to hold on to the love of your life, then beware jealousy!

kissing (*kiss-ing* verb)
This is a difficult one, isn't it? It is always fraught with "Should I?", "Shouldn't I?", "What will she say?", "What will she think?" Well, of course, it all depends on whether or not she wants you to kiss her, doesn't it?

In the films it all looks so simple, doesn't it? Their eyes meet, everything goes misty, music plays and they kiss, totally missing each other's noses, which is an art in

57

itself. But real life isn't like that, is it? You don't hear music as you kiss, for a start. Unless of course you're in a disco, in which case you don't hear anything else. So how can you tell if it's *right*? If it's That Moment? I'm not sure. All I can really say is you'll probably just *know*. But be careful. When you look into her eyes and see that far-away look, make sure it really is The Moment, and not just the fact that she's forgotten to put in her contact lenses!

love (*luv* noun)
Billions upon billions of words have been written about love. What it feels like, what it means, what it costs. Entire rain forests have been sacrificed on the altar of man's (and woman's) curiosity about love. But no-one has ever really defined what it is. And this book is no exception.

machismo (*match-izz-mo* noun)
Arnold Schwarzenegger has got it. Dolf Lundgren has got it. Sylvester Stallone has got it, although he probably has to tie it on. So, what is it? It's that essential Male Quality. A quality that we are told all girls go for, and all blokes want. Obviously the reason blokes want it is because they believe the stuff about all girls going for it. But do all girls go for it? Or is it just a rumour put about by blokes who took up weightlifting when they got bored with stamp collecting, and then didn't know what to do with it?

Well, whatever the truth is, I can tell you that qualities like humour and machismo, are not things that you can develop, like muscles. You either have these qualities or you don't. Oh yes, naturally you can develop muscles, but if you haven't got machismo, you'll just be a weed with thick arms. The trick is not to worry about it. You'll find someone who loves you for yourself ... eventually!

music (*moo-sick* noun)
Music is something that plays an enormous rôle in the lives of all of us. Not only is it a great source of enjoyment, but it also provides us with rôle models. And here I'm not really referring to the "pop stars" them-selves, although they do attract a reasonable number of "wannabees". I'm really thinking about the images contained in the songs.

The Beatles once sang: "She was just seventeen, you know what I mean, and the way she looked was way beyond compare." Does that girl sound like anyone you've ever met, or even seen through a telescope? It'd be a bit more realistic if they'd sung: "The way she looked was way beyond compare apart from just a hint of unsightly nasal hair."

Unrealistic images can build up unnecessary hopes in the minds (and hearts) of prospective boyfriends. The same is true of the blokes in songs. They always sweep the girl off her feet, don't they? They never go to kiss the girl but cock it up, do they? Lyricists never write stuff like: "He swept her up in his arms, her heart went pit-a-pat, but then his toupee fell off as he removed his hat." They never tell you that the hero of the song was a great bloke apart from his personal problem. The heroine never forgets to turn up for a date, or washes her hair instead, does she? The songwriters have got a lot to answer for.

nice (*nice* adjective)
The great conversation stopper, employed by all girls at one time or another.

It's hard to tell whether they do it on purpose or not. But I believe they do. I think you must assume that girls are far more devious than they appear. After all, nobody could be that stupid all the time, could they? (Only joking, girls! Here! What are you doing reading this half of the book? Get back to your own half!) So, if it is a

devious ploy, what does it mean? Nothing. Probably.

This is something else you will come to realize about girls. Not only do many of the things that they do *appear* to have no rational explanation, they do *in fact* have no rational explanation. It's all part of the female mystique. Most blokes are so obvious you can read them like a book, and a Junior Reader at that, whereas most girls are more difficult to fathom than the plot of *Twin Peaks*.

over-enthusiasm (*oh-veren-thoozy-azzem* noun)
In any dealings with the opposite sex, over-enthusiasm is a complete non-starter. It just doesn't work. You need to remain aloof, particularly in what they laughingly call "affairs of the heart". Girls do not like to be rushed for any reason. So, the key is . . . be cool. Oh. Perhaps it *does* exist after all!

passes (*parsez* noun plur.)
If you're thinking: "Oh, I've got one of them! For the bus!", then I would hazard a guess that you are about as far away from coping with girls as anyone could ever be. Because naturally I am not referring to any form of cut-price travel permit. I am referring to the means by which members of the opposite sex indicate that they are interested in each other. The things that men don't make to girls in glasses, etc.

So, how do we indicate our attraction to each other? The girls, I have to say, have got this one taped. They employ the old Note from a Friend ploy. It's the human equivalent of a baboon's red bottom. This is how it works:

Girl A gets girl B (her best mate) to write a note to the boy of her dreams and stick it in his desk. You, the object of her affections (oh, come on! You must be the object of someone's affections!) read the note, which is anonymous, although the best mate usually forgets and signs it. Nevertheless, it works. Simple!

So why don't we blokes use this method? Well, mainly because it *is* so simple. And as we know, being men of the world and generally more worldly wise than your average girl (or so we like to think), we know that simple things go wrong very quickly. I mean, look at Nosher Jenkins! He was simple, and he went wrong within six months of leaving school.

And anyway, we prefer to do our own dirty work. If we fancy someone, we prefer to let them know ourselves, subtly, without half the school finding out. Just in case it goes wrong. And so we enter into an endless round of little looks, winks and nudges, safe in the knowledge that eventually it'll work. She'll notice. And even after we've been carted off to the funny farm, we're still convinced that we were right. And of course, if she comes to visit, we'll <u>*know*</u> that we were right! And if she doesn't . . . well, it's one less person to pinch the grapes!

A SIMPLE PASS

quiet (*cuyert* noun)

Ah! What a quality! If you are, for instance, an only child, you'll know that joy of quiet. No-one arguing with you. No-one invading your space. Even if you've got a brother, you'll be aware that the quiet times between the pitched battles are precious to you both. He understands. But after all, he's a boy too, isn't he? Then your mum suddenly announces that you're going to have a little sister. Won't that be nice? Study that word *quiet*. Touch it. It feels good. Kiss it goodbye.

romance (*rome-ants* noun.)

Some people you talk to would have you believe that romance is dead. But it isn't. It's just got a heavy cold at the moment.

Women are meant to be more romantic than men. But are they? Think of the most romantic thing you've ever done, then think of the most romantic thing a girl has ever done. Yes. They are.

But blokes aren't really supposed to be romantic, are they? I mean, if we start making these little romantic gestures, won't everyone think we've gone a bit funny? The answer is this: If you feel the need to make a romantic gesture towards a female, but are worried that it might tarnish your image, then go ahead and do it, but don't let on that it was you. That way no-one will know it was you, and . . . er . . . it'll be a complete waste of time!

sisters (*sis-terz* noun plur)
It is probably hard to believe, but it is a fact that small sisters are just young women covered in jam. One day they will grow up, assuming that they manage to survive the various traps you dream up for them, and prove the wisdom of my words. Of course, if you've got an older sister, you'll already know that I'm telling the truth.

But sisters can be a blessing, albeit a very mixed one. Imagine the situation: you have a sister two years older than you and another one two years younger. (I realize that this sounds a bit like the plot of the worst horror film Hollywood could dream up, but it's just a "for instance", so don't start having nightmares about it.) Now, throughout your early childhood, these sisters will gang up on you and make your whole existence pure hell. Not only your life, but the lives of all your mates as well. They can't really help it, it's the way they're made. Sugar and spice they are not! But then you reach that strange period of your life when, despite strong resistance on your part (and even possibly a doctor's note) you start to notice *girls*. And this is where the mixed blessing bit comes in. Your sisters will always be ugly. They can't help that, they were born like it. But their friends! Suddenly they look very attractive. They can't be! It must be the light playing a nasty trick on you. No. It isn't. They really do look pretty good. What's more, they know that you've noticed. That's fine. That's the blessing bit. The mixed bit is the fact that your sisters have noticed too. And boy oh boy! Are they ever going to let you forget it? Not on your life!

teasing (*tea-zing* verb)
Teasing takes many forms. One form is the net result of the situation outlined above. The merciless ribbing by your sisters about the fact that you find their friends attractive.

Far worse than this is the teasing reserved for the first boy in a group to start noticing that girls are different. Up until this moment you have all agreed that all girls are stinky smelly. You all know this to be a fact, even though none of you have ever been closer than about thirty yards to one. Then, all of a sudden, overnight almost, one by one you start to realize that they aren't. In fact, they might almost be real people, if that's at all possible.

Well, of course, if you were all to realize this at precisely the same moment, there wouldn't be a problem. But you don't. No! That Great Superpower in the Sky has yet again arranged things badly as far as blokes are concerned. (And they reckon He's one of the lads! I reckon He's a woman with a stick-on beard.) Anyway, if you happen to be the first in the group to say: "Hang on! I don't think them girl things is all that bad, really. In fact . . ." Stop right there, if you value your dignity even slightly! Because if you don't the teasing will be merciless. And boy oh boy! can chaps be cruel!

unisex (*yoony-seckz* noun)
Very much a thing of the late Seventies/early Eighties, unisex was presumably seen as a way of introducing an element of equality into our everyday lives. But in reality it's just another way of humiliating us poor blokes. For example:
Unisex lavatories: In some countries this basically means that men and women use the same entrance door, but then go about their business in separate areas. Not so in this country. Not in my experience, anyway. In this country unisex lavatories basically mean that as you're using the urinal stall, an elderly female cleaner will suddenly appear, smoking, whistling and mopping round your feet. Very off-putting!
Unisex hairdressers: Again not entirely what the name suggests, but rather a golden opportunity for Tracy, Sharon and the rest of the staff at *Hair-Raisers Unisex Hair Salon* to have a bit of a giggle at the sight of you dressed in a pink floral overall that is several sizes too small. If you say anything, they murmur apologetically: "It's the largest one we have, sir!" Rubbish! There's a woman sitting opposite wearing exactly the same gar-

ment, and she's at least the size of Cornwall. It's simply a ploy to make blokes look silly. Dreamed up by a girl, I'll bet! But what can you do about it? Simple! Go to the local barber's instead.

vulgarity (*vull-gary-tee* noun)
How many times have you heard someone say: "Not in front of the ladies"? It's OK, I don't want to know the exact amount. But this is what some men say. Actually, there are double standards at work here, because a bunch of blokes will get together and start telling the filthiest stories imaginable (and some that aren't imaginable), and if a female walks in the room, they immediately clam up. It becomes a case of "not in front of the ladies". You see, there's this theory that girls/women/ladies don't like vulgar talk. Which is all right and proper. A lot of men don't like vulgar talk, either. However, I am reliably informed that when it comes to being rude, girls can be much worse than boys, as long as there are no members of the opposite sex present, of course. I wonder if it's true? There's really no way of finding out, not even by going to a unisex lavatory!

weddings (*wed-dingz* noun plur)
"The greatest moment in a girl's life", so they say. Funny, they never seem to say that it's the greatest moment in a bloke's life, do they? But it should be. After all, he's finally getting the girl of his dreams. But if you look around at weddings the blokes always look rather haunted, don't they? Have you noticed that? That strange motley group of cousins that you didn't even know you had. All huddled in a corner, wondering which one's going to be next.

It's enough to put you off for life, isn't it? Particularly when you're still young, and girls are a mystery to you. There you are, you've only just started liking girls after years of wondering what they were doing on earth at all, and suddenly all the men in the room are behaving as if the worst possible thing that could ever happen to anyone is that they should get married to one.

So why do they do it? They do it for love. And that's why the Motley Cousins are all looking haunted. Because they know, deep down, that one day they too will do exactly the same thing!

X-girlfriend (*ex-girlfriend* noun)
This obviously refers to any girl who was once the object of your affections, but no longer is. (I'm not including the cute little six-year-old whom you shared your trifle with at that party all those years ago, I'm referring to any girl who's been "dumped" by you).

However, it may dent your ego just a little to realize that girls probably cope with becoming "X" better than boys. I know you were secretly hoping you'd left a trail of broken hearts behind you, but I think it's unlikely, somehow. You see, girls generally get more attention from the opposite sex than boys do. And, although they are choosier about whom they go out with, that attention can be a great morale-booster when you're on the rebound. When a fella gets dumped people generally start to wonder what's wrong with him. One day they all think you're a Rolls Royce, the next you're a Lada. Hey-ho! Such is life!

I'M AN EX-REBOUND OF HERS

youthclubs (*yoofclubz* noun plur)
Youthclubs, in fact clubs of all descriptions, are great places to meet girls (except boys' clubs. Boys' clubs are lousy places to meet girls). Mainly because you are under no pressure. If you want to chat to girls, then you can. If you'd rather play table tennis, then you've had it 'cos there's only one bat and the table's broken.

Unfortunately you'll always get the little cluster of people (of both sexes) who are only there for the dates

(dates with the opposite sex, I mean. Not boxes with "Produce of Turkey" written on the top). This does tend to put a blight on the proceedings if you've only gone along for a quiet game of Mah Jong (sorry! Mah Jong's off unless you don't mind playing with half the tiles missing).

But if you are "only there for the spare" (spare girls, that is) then you can put on your gladrags (school uniform with a different jacket and tie) and strut your funky stuff (and other "right-on" expressions!).

There is, however, a word of warning that you would do well to heed. That is, when a bunch of lads get together and start peacocking it in front of a bunch of girls with the express purpose of impressing those girls, particularly if they are trying to be "cool" (which we've more or less established doesn't exist), it very often has the opposite effect. So be warned, lads!

zips (*zipz* noun plur)
I read somewhere that Lord Mountbatten invented the zip fly, proving quite conclusively (if proof were needed) that Royalty have far too much time on their hands. I am not suggesting that zips are a bad thing generally speaking, but they have a life of their own, not to mention a logic of their own, which certainly leads me to believe that the original zip was probably thought up by a woman. Why do I say this? Well, think about it:

You've arranged a date. Unfortunately, you've arranged it for the same evening as your Venture Scouts meeting. That's not a problem. Scouts finishes at eight, you're meeting her at eight-thirty. The only problem is that she doesn't know you're in the Scouts. Now, there's nothing wrong with the Scouts, but some people, you know, think it's a bit train-spottery. Best to keep quiet about it. So, you've taken along a change of clothes, and you've got half an hour to switch from Right Old Dib-Dobber to Right-On Dude! So, what happens? The zip sticks, doesn't it? It's almost as though the Venture Scouts trousers are saying: "Go on! Tell her you're a Scout! What's the matter, embarrassed or something?"

Now, it is possibly a little unfair to blame the female race in situations like this, but the mere fact is that the zip stays firmly put in every other situation other than those involving your trying to impress a girl, and I cannot believe that it is pure coincidence. Oh, no. A devious mind has had a hand in it somewhere along the line. And I bet that hand is wearing nail varnish!

STOP!
ON NO ACCOUNT MOVE PAST THIS POINT.

OH, ALL RIGHT THEN, IF YOU MUST-BUT WATCH OUT YOU DO SO AT YOUR OWN RISK! *

TURN THE BOOK AROUND UNTIL IT'S UPSIDE DOWN...

NOW CLOSE THE BOOK AND START READING, 'COPING WITH BOYS'

* PROBABLE BRAIN DAMAGE

Coping WITH BOYS

Kara May

Illustrated by Martin Brown

Hippo Books
Scholastic Children's Books
London

Scholastic Children's Books,
Scholastic Publications Ltd,
7–9 Pratt Street, London NW1 0AE, UK

Scholastic Inc.,
730 Broadway, New York, NY 10003, USA

Scholastic Canada Ltd,
123 Newkirk Road, Richmond Hill,
Ontario, Canada L4C 3G5

Ashton Scholastic Pty Ltd,
PO Box 579, Gosford, New South Wales,
Australia

Ashton Scholastic Ltd,
Private Bag 1, Penrose, Auckland 6,
New Zealand

Text copyright © Peter Corey, 1992
Illustrations © Martin Brown, 1992

ISBN 0 590 55044 6

Made and printed by Cox & Wyman, Reading, Berks

Typeset by Goodfellow & Egan

10 9 8 7 6 5 4

Forewords...[1]

This is a book about girls and boys. It is *for* girls and boys. One half is for boys. One half is for girls.

Boys, please note: you are now approaching the half reserved for girls only.

We'll do a deal, fellas: you stay out of our half and we'll stay out of yours. To get to your half this is what you do:

Stand on your head to send the blood to your brain (and I'm giving you full credit for having one), then read the following three times:

1. Close the book.
2. Hold the book in your right hand and turn it full circle with your left. The book should now look upside-down, which indeed it is.
3. Turn the book towards you. Keep turning till you can read the words: *Coping With Girls*.

This brings you to your half of the book, and I urge you to read it. The way your sex has coped with ours over the past 7000 years or so (see *History of the World*) has been, how can I describe it? The word that leaps to mind is "heavy-footed", i.e. to trample us underfoot.[2] So on

---

1. If they came at the back of the book they'd be backwords, but because they come before the back they're forewords.
2. And it's a good day (for us) when you're wearing your trainers instead of your Doc Marten's.

behalf of girls the world over, I'm crossing my fingers you'll find new ways and means of coping with us. Because we're coming up with new ways and means of coping with you! That's just one of the topics discussed in our half of the book.[1]

So, back to your own half, fellas (see instructions above). What follows is *strictly for girls*.

Okay, girls. That's got rid of the boys. We can loosen up, open up and talk about what we talk about when there are no boys around with their big ears flapping.[2] They don't know it, but you and I know that Number 1 on our list of Talking Points isn't homework or how tigers got their spots but Boys. Well, they're a fact of life, aren't they? A fact that causes us aggro (see *aggro*),

1. We're the Fair Sex, so we we're not hogging all the book. All we want is an equal share of it.
2. Any boy who dares to venture beyond this point, be warned! You may not like what you find.

the jitters, embarrassment (see *embarrassment*) and lots of other things we could do without.

BUT, if you could wave a magic wand and remove boys from the planet, would you do it? Yes or No?
I've asked myself the question a million times. I also put it to countless girls the world over. The voting was as follows:

YES – no votes.

NO – every vote.

Which says something about us. Right? Like we're crazy? But then, no one's perfect, are they?

Since history began it's been Boys v Girls, i.e. The (mostly) Fair Sex v The (mostly) Foul. Battles come and go but the Battle of the Sexes goes on and on, which isn't surprising, now I come to think of it, since it seems we don't want an all-out victory with boys irrevocably removed from the planet. But we don't want to be trampled on either, or have our brains poured down the kitchen sink, and we *do* want our share of any cake that's going, before it's gobbled up by a brawny/goofy/snotty or any other type of boy.

What *do* we do? How *do* we cope? I've spent years of my life trying to find out.

I began by investigating us and How to Cope with Being a Girl, then I took a close look at various varieties of them, i.e. Parents, Society at Large and Marilyn Pinkerton. I was just thinking about what to study next when I remembered something my History teacher[1] said one brilliantly sunny day, when everyone in the class was looking through the window watching the birds, bees and butterflies, while Snoddy droned on about the Great Fire of London.

1. His name was Mr Snodgrass/Snoddy/Snods. Remember it. You'll be meeting him again.

"They put it out hundreds of years ago. What's it got to do with now?" someone (me) asked.

Snoddy scratched his bald patch and sucked his teeth (a sure sign that words of wisdom *à la* Snod were coming next), and said: "The past teaches us about the present."

"Teaches us what?"

Simple question, huh? But Snoddy thought it was impertinent and sent me to stand in the corridor.

I took the opportunity to finish the packet of crisps I'd only partly demolished in History when the Head came along and caught me with my mouth full . . . but that's another story. Back to the past. I took a quick look at it and learned that boys, then as now, had grubby necks and filthy feet and were dirtier fighters. But the past is dead. So I quickly buried it before it began to

smell, and went on to make an in-depth study of the different types of boys we have to cope with today.

If you've tried to lift it you'll have realized that this is a heavy book. The weightiest part of it is an A to Z of coping with boys in tight corners, embarrassing circumstances and the downright awkward situations they get girls into given half a chance. For every problem a boy might try to dump on your doorstep, your head or wherever he sees the opportunity, you'll find suggested ways and means of how to cope. They've been thoroughly tried and tested either by myself or by other girls

NOW WHERE DID I PUT THAT BOOK?

who've been there before you, and carry a Safety Guarantee.

NB Surprise is a boy's most devastating tactic. Be prepared for any eventuality and carry this book with you at all times.

Coping with being a girl.....

Being a girl is our first experience of life. By the time we bounce into the world we've had nine months to get used to it and from then on we just go on being what we are, a girl. No problem. No problem? Ah, well, yes, but . . . by now you'll have had enough Life Experience to know somehow it doesn't work out like that!

I wanted to start writing this book where most of us start, so I set off with my typewriter to a maternity hospital.[1] It was a unisex hospital and newborn girls and boys were put in the same ward. The boys had blue bows tied to their cots and a label that read:

I'M A BOY![2]

The girls' cots were decked out in puke-pink ribbons. On their labels were the words:

IT'S A GIRL!

IT ??????!!!!

1. The Stork and Gooseberry Bush Maternity Hospital, Yowling Road, Nappeeton.
2. You'll have already worked it out, so there's no need for me to tell you the boys don't write it themselves – someone else does it for them.

8

Starting life as an IT is a problem boys don't have to cope with. You'd think they'd be grateful and count their blessings. But no!

Take Tony-Next-Door.[1] He's forever bleating on about how tough it is being a boy because boys' parents have 'expectations'.

Coping with parents

Tony likes to spend Saturdays curled up with a book or playing his flute, but his parents expect him to play football. "It's what my dad did and your dad did. It's what boys do and we expect you to do it," says his mum.

But compare Tony's plight with Wendy's. Wendy's parents expect her to spend Saturdays window-shopping or painting her toenails. "It's what your mum did when she was a girl. I expect no less from you," says her dad.

1. Take him with a pinch of salt and a dollop of ketchup and you'll find him easier to swallow.

I WISH SHE'D TAKE UP THE FLUTE

But Wendy wants to spend Saturdays playing rugby. She's got the legs and shoulders for it and, to use her own words, she's a born rugger player. But her parents have pointed out that she was born a girl. They took her rugby boots to Oxfam, gave her a shopping bag and a bottle of nail varnish and told her to start painting.

I know at least fifty boys who spend Saturdays with a book or a musical instrument, but I don't know any girls who play rugby on Saturdays or any other day. Which proves that parents are tougher on girls and stick to their expectations, but give in to boys and let them do as they want.

It's not only parents who have their expectations. Society at Large has them too. Until not so long ago it expected girls to be little women, i.e. to stay at home and

cook and sew and flit round the castle/house/hovel wielding a feather duster. You might feel things haven't changed, but they have. The price girls have to pay today for doing things males think only males should do isn't as high as it was. I can give a money-back guarantee that if you decide a military career is You, you won't be bound hand and foot and burned to a crisp at the stake. Which is what happened to the Maid of Orleans, Joan of Arc,[1] when she decided to join the army rather than stay at home minding her dad's sheep.[2]

ZE EQUAL OPPORTUNITIES COMMISSION WILL HEAR OF ZIS

Of course being a girl today is far from easy. But it's easier than it was and it *could* be easier than it is.

If the boys weren't miles away in their own half of this book, I wouldn't say what I'm going to say. Girls should stick together. Yes? Yes. But do we? . . .

Coping with other girls

As a girl, it wasn't my parents or even Society at Large that made me wish the earth would swallow me up and put me out of my misery – it was Other Girls. Marilyn Pinkerton in particular. Marilyn's trainers were always

1. Born 1412 Burned 1431
2. She was allergic to wool.

the latest of the latest. What was the problem with that? The problem was *my* trainers were always at least three months out of date.

Marilyn had all the things I wanted and hadn't and hadn't the things I didn't want but had . . . like the zit on my chin, a permanent fixture that wouldn't go away no matter how hard I squeezed. *Her* parents let her out any time whereas *mine* only let me out on Saturdays *if* I'd given them a minute-by-minute account of what I was going to do, where I was going to do it and who with. (Even then it was no pocket money for a week if I wasn't home by ten.) Marilyn had more girlfriends than me, and as for boyfriends . . . I tried to count how many she had but stopped when I ran out of fingers. A monkey who couldn't count could have counted my boyfriends because I didn't have any – not one, or a half or a quarter or one-sixteenth of one.

Then, one day, when Marilyn was peering down her perfectly straight (mine turned up) nose at my out-of-date trainers, I flipped. I let it all come out about how I had no nails left because I'd bitten them to the bone because she made me feel a creep, a nothing, a nobody.

I thought Marilyn was going to faint. But she pulled up her (designer silk) blouse and showed me the rash she said I'd brought her out in because I was always going on about how my parents were better than hers because they made me stay in and do my homework and how I didn't need to wear designer gear to show I was Somebody. And then she told me *she* had nightmares that *I'd* find out she plastered her face with make-up to cover up her 20,000 spots, whereas I could go for the natural look because I had only one (little) zit.

By then I was the one reeling with shock, and I was almost a terminal case when she said she paid girls to be

her friends, in chocolate bars and Lycra tights, and she paid her boyfriends too, but not with Lycra tights.

I looked at Marilyn. Marilyn looked at me. We started to giggle, and when girls giggle together they become best mates and that's what happened to us. I can't promise that the girl who makes you feel a worm may secretly feel a worm too. But it's simple to find out: ask her.

Coping with Other Girls, Society at Large and Parents *and* starting life as an IT is a headache. If you've got a headache now, please lie down for half an hour. You need to be fighting fit to cope with what's coming next: the knobbly-kneed bipeds who borrow your best biro then won't give it back: boys.

Girls have had to cope with boys since history began. How did it begin and how have girls through history coped? Let's dig up the past and find out.

Coping through history..

HOW IT ALL BEGAN

In the beginning there weren't any tabloid newspapers to report on what was going on in the world. In fact there wasn't a world until an Almighty Male called God[1] created it and all the creatures in it. The last of the creatures He made was a man called Adam, who bore a strong resemblance to the ape. "He's my first attempt at a human," thought God. "I'll have another go." He couldn't be bothered to start again from scratch so he decided to make the improved version out of Adam's rib.

THIS CAN'T BE RIGHT

"Out of my rib!" squawked Adam.

He was so terrified he fell to the ground in a faint (no man has been brave enough to give birth since).

1. Who created God? Only God knows – and so far, He's not telling.

When he came to, however, it was all over and he saw another human standing beside him.

"She's a woman," said God. "Her name is Eve." Eve's body curved gracefully, her face wasn't hairy and she had no knobbles on her knees. "I have to say, Adam, she's a definite improvement on you," said God.

God put Adam and Eve in the Garden of Eden, a place of great beauty where the sun always shone, lions and lambs snuggled up together and mosquitoes didn't bite. He told them they could live there in everlasting bliss. "All I ask in return is that you don't eat that apple." He pointed to a nearby tree with a large red apple on it.

"Aye, aye, God. Whatever you say," said Adam.

But Eve was curious. "Why can't we eat it?"

"Because if you do you'll find out all sorts of things you'd wish you hadn't. All I want is for you to be happy. I'll do everything for you," said God, "and give you everything you need. You won't have to worry about a thing."

God was as good as His word. They didn't have to work, grow their food or cook it. If they fancied a hamburger and chips with lashings of ketchup, there it was on a porcelain plate (no plastic in Paradise).

"It's P for Perfect," said Adam.

"Mmm . . .", said Eve. Eden *was* perfect, but . . .

What the "but" was, she couldn't quite work out. She had a feeling it was something to do with the apple, and time and again she found herself wondering what she'd find out if she ate it.

"Go on, Eve. Take a bite. You know you want to." Eve looked down to find a snake in the grass beside her.

"But God said I'd regret it."

"He could be wrong!" said the snake, and slithered off.

15

Eve couldn't wait to tell Adam about her conversation with the snake. But he got very uppity and reminded her that God had told them ignorance was bliss and that was good enough for him.

"But I want find out for myself," said Eve.

"God said we mustn't," said Adam.

"God mightn't find out. It's a risk we'll have to take. Please, Adam, please. Just a little bite!"

"Well, all right," said Adam. "But just a little bite."

Together they picked the apple.

Together they took a bite.

A roar came from above. "Ungrateful wretches!"

God came storming down on a thunderbolt and

EITHER WE'VE MADE A TERRIBLE MISTAKE EATING THAT APPLE OR GOD'S INVENTED SURFING

ranted on about how He'd given them Paradise but that wasn't enough – they wanted His apple as well. He pointed to Eve's tummy, which had begun to swell.

"You've found out how to make children, but knowledge doesn't stop there! Don't say I didn't warn you!"

He hurled them out of Eden and bolted the gate behind them.

Adam and Eve had to fend for themselves in a very different world beyond. All too soon they found out all sorts of things they wished they hadn't and Adam never stopped moaning.

"In Eden I didn't know what it was like to be cold or hungry or have the toothache! I didn't know what it was like to be sad or sick, let alone dead."

"You're not dead yet!" Eve reminded him.

"It's only a matter of time. I could have lived for all eternity in Paradise if you hadn't made me eat God's apple."

"Oh, so I rammed it down your throat, did I?"

"I only ate it to shut you up. It's all your fault."

"No, it's not!"

"Yes, it is!"

Angry words hurtled through the air. And soon pots and pans and the baby's rattle went hurtling after. They'd never rowed in Paradise, but now they couldn't stop.

To her dying day Eve never let on that she felt guilty about not having the nerve to eat the apple on her own, and the part she'd played in getting Adam thrown out of Eden.

And Adam never let on that he felt a failure because it hadn't entered his mind to risk disobeying God, and Eve had thought of eating the apple first. It was a wound to his pride and it hurt. He was scared Eve would find out

and make fun of him, so he acted big, squashed her whenever he could and when she said she didn't like being sat on, sang the only song he knew: "It's all your fault we're not in Eden."

Whatever the rights and wrongs of it, if Adam and Eve had done as God had told them they'd still be prancing innocently about in Paradise, the Battle of the Sexes wouldn't have started, and you and I wouldn't be here. Well, that's how the story goes ...

THE ANCIENT EGYPTIANS

Very ancient Egypt was the first equal-sex society (and the last, for thousands of years). Girls and boys had the same right to own a cow and to inherit money. When a girl married, she didn't have to give her cow or her money to her husband. She could keep what was hers, he could keep what was his, or they could share it out (equally) between them.

Evidence of women's equal status can be found not only in the very ancient Egyptians' inscribed-in-stone laws, but in a stone-made monument called The Sphinx. The Sphinx has the body of a lion (to remind both sexes of their (equally) animal origins) and a unisex head: in other words, it could be a man, it could be a woman, it depends on how you look at it.

As you'd expect, where women were rated as equals the society thrived. The arts and sciences flourished. Even the building industry boomed and they built houses not only for the living, but also for the dead, i.e. pyramids.

But, as time went by, and very ancient Egypt became ancient Egypt, the first male wound (see *How it all began*) started playing up again and men began to throw their weight around to prove to themselves they were top dog, cock of the walk, pharaoh of the pyramid, etc. Rather than cause bloodshed and injury to their boyfriends, husbands, fathers, sons and the little chap who delivered the milk, the women didn't fight back. Maybe they should have. Run by men only, the once-great nation fell into a decline. Then a queen called Cleopatra decided the rot had gone far enough.

Cleopatra was kind and warm-hearted. She agreed to give the lads a second chance and let them help in restoring the country to its former glory. But Mark and Julius started squabbling over who was to carry her lunchbox ... although she'd issued a public statement that she could carry it herself. The outcome was that Julius got stabbed, Anthony got shot and Cleopatra was left holding the asp.[1]

For Egypt, it's been downhill ever since.

1. A poisonous snake, possibly the same one that tempted Eve in Eden.

THE ANCIENT GREEKS

Remember Snodgrass (see p. 5)? If an Ancient Greek had walked into our classroom, Snods would have kissed the hem of his Ancient toga. He had a grovelling awe and admiration for the Ancient Greeks and was forever babbling on about how civilized they were and how grateful we should be to them because they'd invented democracy.

Civilized? Democratic? See what you think.

Helen was a young beauty married to Menelaus, a very ancient Greek with rotting teeth, a paunch and a bald head. (The marriage was arranged by her parents.)

One day Paris came to stay. He was young and heart-stoppingly handsome and the inevitable happened – Paris and Helen fell for each other and ran away to Troy together. Menelaus was so enraged he got his toga in a twist and persuaded his brother, King Agamemnon, to go to war with Troy and fetch Helen back. But the ships couldn't sail because the wind wouldn't blow and Agamemnon was told it never would unless he sacrificed his daughter by taking her to a cliff and having her throat cut. So that's what he did. Soon after that the wind began to blow, and the Greeks sailed off to fight one of the bloodiest wars in history.[1]

---

1. If Agamemnon had bothered to listen to the weather forecast, he'd have found out the wind was due to blow that day anyway, and saved himself a daughter.

I stopped yawning to ask Snods what was so civilized about an old man going to war over a young wife who'd been forced to marry him the first place, or a father who'd sacrificed his daughter to make the wind blow. But Snods gave me his look that said, You're a girl, you wouldn't understand. And he's right. And as for Ancient Greek democracy . . . Guess who could vote in it? Men only! FEMALES KEEP OUT was written all over the voting booths and any female who didn't was sent to the salt mines.

If that's democracy, Snoddy's a Martian. Which, now I come to think of it . . .

1. To bring the bloodshed to an end, Helen bravely returned to her revolting old husband.

THE ANCIENT ROMANS AND THE ANCIENT BRITS

The Ancient Romans were the BC technocrats. They had indoor loos and central heating, which was all very well if you were a boy. If you were a girl the odds were you wouldn't live long enough to put your bot on the loo seat. Girls were dispensable. Many were disposed of at birth by being left on a hillside to be eaten by wolves.

The all-male Roman leaders decided to do the world a favour and conquer it so everyone could enjoy the convenience of an indoor loo. One of the countries on their hit list was Ancient Britain.

The Ancient Brits were an assortment of tribes. They didn't have central heating, but they had queens as well as kings and Queen Boadicea headed the Norfolk Tribe. She wanted the Romans out a.s.a.p.[1]

"When I want to go to the loo, I go behind a bush. No more jaw, jaw, jaw! It's war, war, war!"

The kings whinged on about how the Romans had better weapons and there was nothing else to do but surrender.

"We can use our brains," said Boadicea.

While the kings were still looking for theirs, she came up with the idea of sticking blades on the wheels of the chariots, which made mincemeat of the Roman Army.

Alas, Boadicea was killed on the battlefield. Without her leadership the Brits' army crumbled and the Romans took over the country. Like the Egyptians and Greeks

---

1. As Soon As Possible.

before them, where the men thought they knew everything and women knew nothing, they got their comeup-
pance and the once mighty Roman Empire crumbled.

The VIKINGS

The Vikings invaded Britain from Scandinavia, wearing bearskins and helmets with horns on. They were the forbears of Rambo and their treatment of females was on a par with his. Enough said.

24

 # THE FEUDAL AGE

This was the age when the rich and powerful were forever feuding with each other. They burned each other's crops and castles. There wouldn't have been a blade of wheat or a castle left standing if they hadn't decided to do their fighting in someone else's country instead of laying waste to their own.

"It's our duty to go," they told their womenfolk. "You'll have to muddle along till we get back."

Off they went, army after army of them, to fight wars called Crusades in the Middle East.

25

As soon as the last armour-plated soldier was out of sight, the women rolled up their sleeves and set about clearing up the mess the men had left behind them. And I'm not just talking about picking up their dirty socks and putting away their boxer shorts. High-born ladies took over their husbands' huge estates and sent wandering minstrels[1] to inform everyone they were under New Management. The more lowly weeded their husbands' fields and re-planted the cabbage patch.

1. Homeless newscasters who wanted to be pop singers and went round the village singing the news in the hope a talent scout would spot them and give them a record contract.

And if they didn't fancy the country life they worked as shopkeepers, chemists, barbers, traders, artists and armour-makers. They ran the schools. In hospitals they didn't just empty bedpans – they worked as surgeons and doctors. You won't read about this in most history books,[2] but there are pictures that prove it.

But then word got back to the Crusaders of how well women were running things without them, and they caught the first ship home. They pushed women out of their jobs and any woman who complained was burned as a witch. This way of dealing with women who tried to do anything more challenging than peel the spuds continued till the Great Fire-Wood Shortage of 1736, when the Law For Burning Women as Witches was abolished.

---

2. This is because most history books are written by men who suffer from a complicated medical condition that affects their egos. (see *ego*).

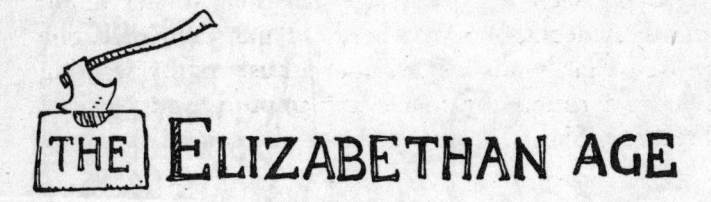 THE ELIZABETHAN AGE

There are three ages in British history named after people. All three are named after women. The first of these was Elizabeth I. Elizabeth's dad, Henry, like our Liz Taylor, was famous for his number of marriages. Unlike Liz, Henry had a brick where his heart should have been, and when he wanted to get rid of a wife quickly, he chopped her head off. This fate befell Elizabeth I's mum, because she didn't produce a son.[1]

1. Which was Henry's fault anyway, because men are responsible for the sex of their children. But he was too ignorant to know that.

Having seen what marriage had done to her mum, Elizabeth decided to keep her head and stay single. She proved a girl's not lost without a husband by walking blindfold round the maze at Hampton Court before breakfast. She also proved that a girl can be as handy

with the axe as her dad and she beheaded her Scottish cousin Mary to stop her getting her hands on her throne.[1] She could have chopped Mary's hands off instead, but Elizabeth had been brought up to believe that Dad's way of doing things was best.

As well as proving things, Elizabeth disproved the man-made myth that women can't handle money. She was especially good at handling other people's, and the country became immensely rich from the booty plundered by her self-appointed pirates (see *Wally*, p. 69). After Elizabeth's death it was frittered away by a series of witless kings, before another queen came along to restore it.

1. This is one of the few examples in history of one girl being mean to another.

The Victorian Age

Queen Victoria was a financial genius who invented a money-making game called "Empire Building". She also had a great sense of humour. When her husband Albert died she tried to see the funny side but she'd lost her glasses and couldn't find it. But she was queen enough to own up. As they lowered Albert's coffin into the grave, Victoria admitted, "We are not amused".

And can you blame her? Her old man left her to bring up nine kids, rule Britain and build the British Empire. Being a single mum with two full-time jobs is no joke!

30

The Suffragettes

After 2000 years of democracy *à la Greque* (see *Ancient Greeks*, p. 20) women decided they'd suffered enough and demanded the vote. Men realized the days of ME! ME! ME! I WANT EVERYTHING FOR ME! were coming to an end, but they weren't giving in without a fight. But the women weren't giving in either. They chained themselves to the railings, leaving men to cook their own dinners and make their own beds. They couldn't cope. In 1914 they surrendered and women won the vote. And that was just the start of . . .

WOMEN'S LIBERATION (LIB)

When my gran was a girl and said she wanted Liberation, her boyfriend (now my Grandad) thought she was talking about the perfume she wanted for Christmas.

And when she said she was going to ask for the same money he got for working at Burper's Caff on Saturdays, he bet her a penny she wouldn't get it, because girls always got paid less. Grandad won the bet and that's just one of the reasons, Gran says, that she joined the Liberation Movement and helped to move it into the House of Commons where the Libbers moved so fast

other MPs were left gasping for breath. While they were trying to catch it, the Libbers made some changes in the House, which is why today you get the same money in your pay packet for dishing up French fries at Macpoodles as the twit of a boy who does (or tries to do) the same job.[1]

And that moves us on to the not-too-distant-past and one of the first women in it.

Margaret Thatcher was Britain's first woman Prime Minister and the first Prime Minister to be a woman. You may think that's two ways of saying the same thing, but that's what happens when you get into politics.

Some people[2] believe Margaret Thatcher is the re-incarnation of Elizabeth I. This is because of her no-nonsense way of removing ministers who trod on her toes, got up her nose or on her wick or anywhere else she didn't want to them be. Red was her least favourite colour, so she didn't chop their heads off. She did it her way and either threw the Wets[3] headfirst out of her Cabinet or gave them a bash with her handbag. Her handbag always had an iron in it in case she needed to give her blouse a quick press and she was known the world over as the Iron Lady.

1. Act for Equal Pay for Equal Work, 1975.
2. I own up, I'm of them.
3. A Minister who went out in the rain without an umbrella.

And now we've reached *the present*, which you know as much about as anyone. Write your own version, send it to Snods and he'll give you a mark for it. On second thoughts, don't bother. He usually lit his pipe with my history essays and he'll probably do the same with yours.

WARNING: We're moving into Boy-Infested Territory here. Before proceeding further, put on your sunglasses, gas-mask and bullet-proof vest.

What is a boy?

So that we know what to avoid, we must first decide what a boy *is*. And there we hit our first problem. I've come across little boys at kindergarten who strut about the playground and think they're men. And I've seen men with paunches hanging out of their tracksuits who jog around the park on Sundays (puff, puff! pant pant!) in the mistaken belief they're still boys.

But if we don't know *exactly* what they are, rumour has it that boys are made of the following ingredients:

> slugs
>
> snails
>
> puppy dogs' tails

which explains their unruly, slimy behaviour.

My own research reveals that boys fall into one of the following eight-plus-one (see *Wally*, p. 69) types, each with its distinguishing features, habitat, chat-up line, pros (hard to find) and cons (too many to list them all). NB I heard on the grapevine (I can't tell you which one, I promised not to) that the other half of this book accuses girls of not saying what they mean. But of course it's the other way round, a fact that's so well known I've not bothered to give examples to watch out for.

Types of boys

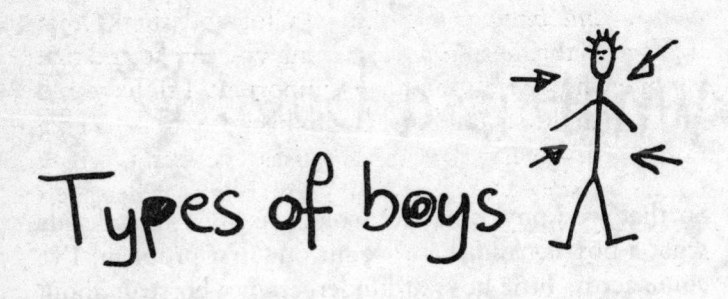

Coping with different types of boys
I: The Yob
Nature and habitat: He's flashy, dressy and a loud-mouth. You'll find him showing off his tonsils on the football terraces or in the school corridor. You can't miss him (unless you flatten yourself against the wall) because he'll be barging down the middle of it with a herd of Yobs like himself.

Chat-up line: "Oi, You!"

Pros and cons: Underneath the Ya-boo yobby bluster, he's a softie. You'll be able to wrap him round your little finger, if that's where you want him. But do you? He eats with his mouth open, belches (loudly) and won't get on with your parents. But if you're not getting on with them either that could be a pro rather than a con.

2: The Brain-Box (also known as the egg-head owing to the shape of his head, which often has a tuft of hair sticking up on top)

Nature and habitat: He thinks a lot and thinks that thinking is the most important thing you can do and that anyone who doesn't think isn't important. I think you'll find him in the school library with his nose stuck in a big book with small print which causes eye-strain, which is the reason why the Brain-Box blinks when he's thinking. I think.

Chat-up line: "I'm a genius."

Pros and cons: You won't need to exercise your mouth by talking – he'll do it all for you. But he'll also shower you with spittle, so remember to wear a mac.

3. The Good-Looking Guy

Nature and habitat: Wow! It's not just the teeth! It's the tan, it's the eyes, it's everything about him. But how do you find him? Join the crowd of girls outside the school gates. He'll be in the middle of it somewhere.

Chat-up line: He doesn't need one. With his looks girls fall at his feet and he picks up the one he likes best.

Pros and cons: He's good to look at. But maybe that's all he's good for.

SWOON
SWOON

FAINT
FAINT

4: The New Age Greenie

Nature and habitat: See the boy standing in the pouring rain in his lunch-break holding a SAVE THE WHALE/DOLPHIN poster? That's the Greenie. He speaks slowly to conserve energy. Recycles other boys' old socks and cast-off jeans by buying clothes at Oxfam. Doesn't eat cows or any other animals. Never goes on a date without a pocket calculator. (See *Pros and cons*).

Chat-up line: "Would you like a leaf of my lettuce?"

Pros and cons: You won't have to convince him you've got a brain and he won't insult you by thinking you can't pay for yourself when you go to the movies. But if it's romance you want, forget the goodnight kiss. He'll be too busy working out your equal share of the cost of shoe leather used in walking you home.

5: The Hulk

Nature and habitat: He's the Tarzan/Rambo lookalike. This chunky lad is living proof of Darwin's theory of evolution, that man is descended from the Ape. You'll find him in the school gym, swinging on a rope.

Chat-up line: "Grunt, Grunt, Grunt!"

Pros and cons: If you're attacked by a bull, you've nothing to fear: he'll grab it by the ears and toss it over his shoulder. If you're an animal lover, you may prefer him to throw you over his shoulder instead. Don't expect him to understand that. The Hulk is a big boy with a small brain.

6: The Knight in Shining Armour

Nature and habitat: Incredibly handsome, polite, charming, strong, brave, adventurous. Gives his life for your slightest whim, likes everything you like, admires you more than any girl in the world, and you can meet him in daydreams and fairy tales.

Chat-up line: "Your wish is my command."

Pros and cons: He's perfect, BUT . . . in the real world he doesn't exist.

7: The Wimp

Nature and habitat: Physical appearances can be deceptive: he may look like a truck driver or like something that crawled out from under a stone. The Wimp bleats rather than speaks, blames others, never himself, and is always on the lookout for a shoulder to cry on. You'll find him on top of his desk when the school hamster escapes or at home, tied to his mum's apron strings.

Chat-up line: "Er, er, er . . ."

Pros and cons: His troubles are always worse than yours and he'll make you feel you were born lucky. But if the ship sinks and there's only one life-belt, you won't be the one who's wearing it!

8: The Nice Guy (or is he?)

Nature and habitat: He smiles a lot, sincerely, and is sincerely interested in what you say, even if it's boring. (You can't be fascinating all the time.) He's the one type of boy who'll borrow your biro and give it back and who'll help his kid sister with her homework. You can find him anywhere in the school doing things no one else would do like tidying up the cloakroom in his free period.

Chat-up line: (*sincerely*) "I think Cliff Richard's brill, don't you?"

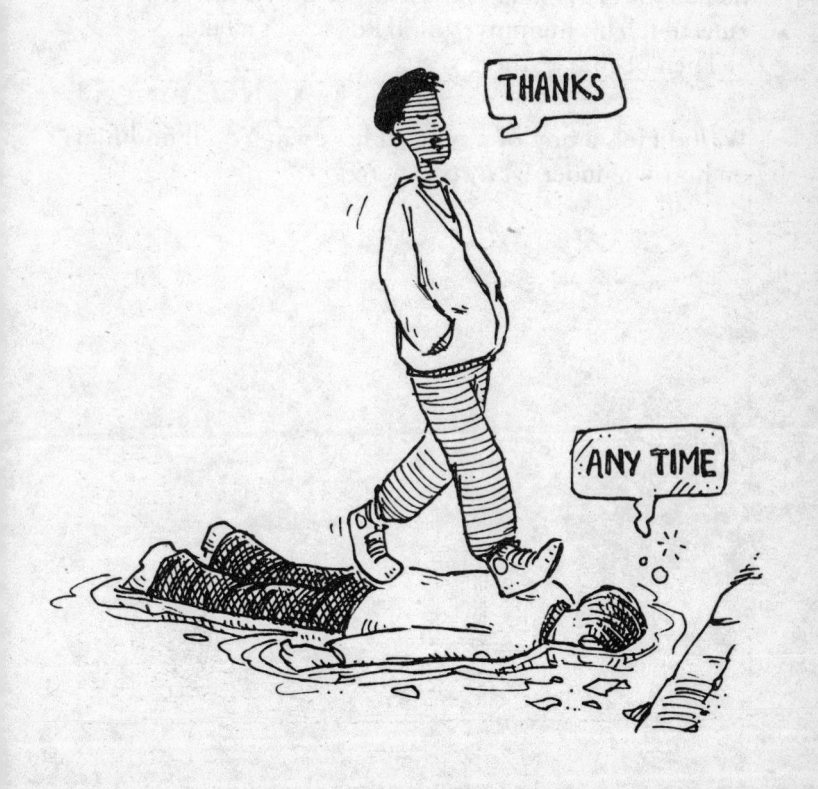

Pros and cons: He won't froth at the mouth or act deaf when you ask him to do you a little favour, like keeping you company while you visit your gran on Cup Final day. But he can keep you awake at night wondering, is he really as nice as he seems? Try this infallible test to find out:

Take that extra-special quartz watch, Walkman or whatever he's been saving up for months to buy and accidentally drop it on something hard like your kid brother's head. If he gives a brave smile and says sweetly, "It's all right, accidents will happen, let's say no more about it," your Nice Guy is genuinely nice. But if he hits the roof (with your head) or bursts into tears and runs to tell his mummy, you'll know he's a fake.

Then of course, there's . . .

Wally: He's a boy of a type all his own. You'll find him on his own under *Wally* (see p. 69)

The A to Z of coping with boys....

Now we know what boys are (sort of), what they're made of and the types they come in. But how do we cope with them?

Curiously, coping with boys doesn't get easier as we get older. Baby girls are able to ignore them altogether and focus their attention on more important matters, like how loudly they need to yell to get Dad to pick their rattle up for the 50,000th time. Then we start school and boys are just the snotty things we don't want to sit next to, and apart from making faces at each other and having competitions to see who can make the biggest splash by jumping in puddles in the school playground, we ignore them and they ignore us and that's the way we like it. But then something goes terribly wrong. This was how it went wrong with me:

I was walking past the Common Room when a boy walked out of it. I'd never seen him before and he was – if I say DIVINE you'll know what I mean. He didn't see me and strode off down the corridor on his (divinely) long legs as if nothing had happened. But something *had* happened – I was having a heart attack or rather, something was attacking my heart. Fearing for my life, I skipped history[1] and hopped off to the Sick Room. I

---

1. And guess who didn't miss me? To find the answer read the earlier part of this part.

told the Doc I'd been suddenly stricken with a desperate longing for a boyfriend. There was something seriously wrong with me (and it wasn't just the funny-looking pie I'd had for lunch). Boys were grubby, snotty twits. In my normal state there was more chance of me riding to the moon on a bicycle than wanting a boyfriend, ever.

I begged her to cure me. "Please, Doc, give me something! Anything!" But she said there wasn't a cure for what I'd got – I'd just have to cope. And most of the time I didn't cope, or not very well, so I'm hoping the A to Z that follows will help you to avoid the pitfalls I stumbled into. Good luck, girls! I hope you cope better than I did!

aaah!

When a boy makes you go "Aaah!" it's for one of three reasons:

1 He's revolting.

2 He's gorgeous.

3 He's trodden on your foot.

If he's revolting, do yourself a favour and don't give him a second look. If he's gorgeous, remember Beauty is Only Skin Deep, take a look at what's underneath before you throw yourself at his feet. And if it's your foot he's trodden on, tread on his.

acne[1]

He's got acne. In case it's escaped his notice, should you point out to him his face is a minefield of flaming spots? Not unless you want to be clobbered with insults. And unless you're a skin specialist with an infallible cure for this unfortunate affliction that turns a boy's skin into a volcanic eruption, offers of remedies will get the same insulting response.

Never come between a boy and his acne. Let them sort it out between them.

1. Girls don't have acne, they have zits. (see p. 71)

adolescent

The adolescent boy is one of the most disruptive and tiresome human species to set his clumsy feet upon the planet. He's unpredictable except in his awfulness, unreliable and so prone to fits of frustrated rage that he can't work out who he is: one moment he thinks he's a two-year-old and wants you to pick up his rattle; the next, he thinks he's a man and watch out anyone who doesn't see things his way!

Native tribes, in their wisdom, round up their adolescent boys and pack them off to a remote place where they can vent their rage on each other. They also set the boys death-defying tasks, such as wrestling with a lion with one hand tied behind their backs and sitting in a bees' nest for a week without flinching, which successfully reduces their number. After a year or two those who've survived are allowed back into the tribe. They return covered in scars and minus a limb or two and, if they're no wiser, even the wildest tearaway is very much subdued.

In our society, alas, adolescent boys are allowed to roam free causing havoc and mayhem. Their parents tear their hair out in despair. Their teachers resign in droves. No one can handle them. No one, that is, except:

THE ADOLESCENT GIRL.

She can give as good as she gets. For a small fee (minimum £50), she will give the benefit of her advice to anyone seeking help on how to handle an adolescent boy, e.g. don't handle him unless you're wearing a decontamination suit, and always have a lump of meat ready to throw at him so he can take a bite at that instead of you.

At the time of writing, the newly formed political

party GKB (Girls Know Best) has a bill before Parliament proposing that Centres for Coping with Adolescent Boys, staffed by AGs (adolescent girls) should be set up throughout the country. This would result in huge savings in tranquillizers for parents and the cost of replacing school carpets where the outrageous behaviour of ABs (adolescent boys) has driven teachers to chewing up the old ones.

aggro
A boy who never causes you aggro (aggravation) is a rare specimen, if not unique. If you come across one, parcel him up and send him to the Natural History Museum, where they'll put him a glass case and preserve him for posterity.

brother (your own)
Your brother is not something you have a choice about. He's inflicted on you by your parents and you may be unfortunate in having more than one.

Brothers operate in the belief that they're sent into the world to cause sisters aggravation (see *aggro*). The big ones do aggravating things like giving a public reading of your *Tell All Diary* in the school playground. The little

49

ones amuse themselves by drawing pictures of themselves on your physics homework in indelible ink.

The natural response is to scream and shout. This isn't advised, so don't do it. It's just what they're hoping you'll do. Acts of vengeance aren't recommended either. You may be justified in tearing your brother slowly limb from limb, boiling him in oil and feeding him to the cat, but injustice being what it is where sisters are concerned, the odds are that you'll be caught by your parents and punished.

The best course is to grit your teeth, hang on to your dignity and ignore your brothers at all times and in all circumstances. Their feeble minds are quickly bored and if you don't give them the satisfaction of watching you lose your rag, they'll soon get bored with trying and leave you in peace.

brother (someone else's)
They are rarely as aggravating as your own. Some of them may be worthy of your friendship or even something deeper . . ..

BROTHERS

YOURS   SOMEONE ELSE'S

crying
If you want a boyfriend to be really rich and famous, make him cry in public – in as public a place as possible. Crying on your shoulder is unlikely to get him on the front pages of the newspaper, so this shouldn't be encouraged. Get him to weep his little heart out where he's sure to be noticed, e.g. on the top of the Eiffel Tower or on a football pitch. But make sure it's a World Cup Final. That way he'll get lots of publicity and make lots of money and be able to buy you that Extra Special Something.[1]

darts
This is a game favoured by boys with thick heads and tiny minds, where a small arrow-shaped feathered missile is thrown at a circular board with a bull's eye in the middle. If he misses, the dart player is liable to see red and charge at whoever's nearest. Make sure it isn't you – always stand well back or wear protective clothing to avoid injury.

dates (edible)
They're a dark brown, sticky fruit, usually eaten at Christmas, stuffed. They should not be confused with the inedible variety (see below).

dates (inedible, with boys)
In common with the edible variety, a date with a boy can leave you wondering why you bothered. On the other hand, it can be surprisingly enjoyable. Alas, there's no

1. A private jet with gold-plated propellers? An island in the sun? A diamond-studded mountain bike? The choice is yours.

certain way of telling one from the other beforehand: the date that you think is going to be sheer heaven can turn out to be a nightmare, while the date you're dreading can turn out to be unadulterated bliss.

Some dates, however, are surefire disasters. Turn them down, always. You don't know how? Try the following:

HIM: I'm only asking you out because the girl I really like turned me down.

YOU: Goodbye! (or more colourful words to that effect).

HIM: If you pay for the seats and buy me a jumbo packet of popcorn, I'll do you a favour and take you to the movies.

YOU: Thanks for the offer, but I can't afford you.

HIM: I'll take you out on a date if you have your hair cut. I don't like girls with long hair.

YOU: I don't like boys with big heads. Cut yours off and I might think about a date.

HIM: I'm going fishing with my mates. You can tag along if you like.

YOU: Wow! Lucky me! Forget it, Buster!

diamonds (see *no*).

discos
Going to a disco is different from going to the dentist's. At least it's meant to be. But a study by the We Love Dentists Society has collected evidence to prove that going to the dentist can be *more* enjoyable than going to a disco, as these three case histories show:
Jackie
Jackie had a new boyfriend called Tom. Their first date was at a disco she'd always wanted to go to, and she was looking forward to it. On arrival, Tom proceeded to jump up and down on her feet with his hefty size elevens. "He wasn't even in time with the music," said Jackie. Tom used her feet as a stamping ground throughout the evening, with the result that every bone in her feet was broken. Jackie spent the next six months in hospital. "I've been put off discos for life," she says. "I'd sooner go to the dentist's."
Paula
Paula was in love with Jason. She'd been longing for a date with him for weeks and then one day, oh joy! he asked her to a disco. He was a brill dancer and spent the evening dancing away with every girl except her. At the stroke of midnight he left with a beautiful girl (not her), leaving Paula to go home alone on the last bus. The agony she suffered, Paula said, was worse than going to the dentist and having all her teeth out.
Aisha
Aisha had never been to a disco and when her friend Katie asked her to go with her, she went along to see what it was like. They were happily bopping together when a herd of orang-utans charged in, all hairy arms and hairy chests. They proceeded to tear to pieces

whatever/whoever they could lay their great big hairy mitts on.

On a terrified second glance the girls realized the intruders were not orang-utans, but football hooligans on the rampage. "We managed to get away through the fire escape but I've never been so terrified in my life," said Aisha. "No more discos for me! It's more scary than going to the dentist."

If you're considering going to a disco, go hoping to enjoy yourself but be prepared for the worst.

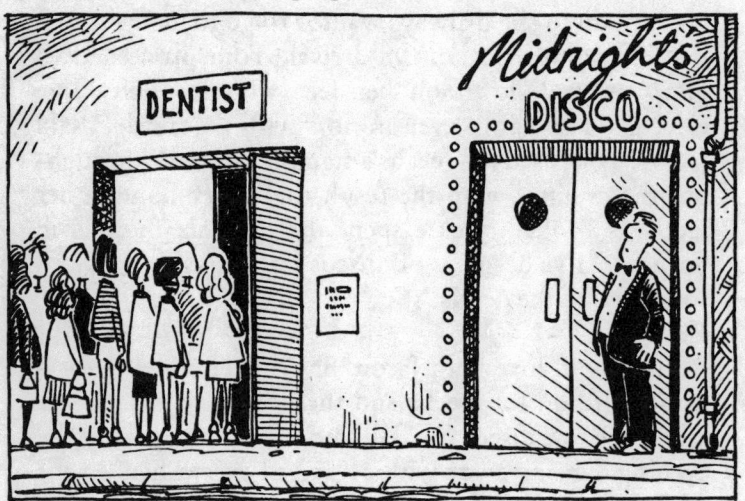

ego

A boy's ego is the part of him he likes best. His ego not only tells him how remarkable (clever, handsome, etc.) he is, it tells the rest of the world as well and runs an advertising campaign on his behalf that begins with the words I AM, followed by a glossy description of what he regards as his assets.

As a consequence, a boy with a big ego is filled with admiration for himself and will expect equally unstinting

admiration from you. Don't expect the same treatment from him. His big ego tells him he's already doing you a big favour by letting you worship at his (usually big) feet.

A boy with a small ego also thinks he's exceptionally handsome/clever/sensitive. But he's too much of a wimp (see wimp) to exercise his tongue to tell you so. Instead, he'll whine and wheedle you into saying he's Mr Gorgeous/Mr Einstein and Second/The Most Sensitive Boy On the Planet. Saying it once won't be enough. He'll want it on a non-stop playing record. And if you're in need of a boost? Forget it. He expects all the ego-boosting for himself.

Your best bet is a boy with a medium-sized ego. These are as common as a unicorn with two horns, so you could have a problem finding one.

embarrassment
First the bad news: at some time or other a boy will cause you embarrassment – it's an experience no girl escapes. The good news is that it's one of the worst experiences you'll ever have to go through. Although you feel you'll die of it at the time, no girl has actually died of embarrassment . . . so far. With a bit of luck you won't be the first.

IT'S ALL LIES I TELL YOU!

For those of you who haven't been through it yet, be prepared. This is the sort of thing you're in for:

A You tell your mum you've met the most wonderful boy on the planet. He's absolutely but absolutely perfect. Your mum can't wait to meet this paragon and he's invited to tea. As soon as he walks through the door your Mr Perfect turns into a moron. He can't string two words together. He picks his nose, slurps his soup and when he gets up, knocks the table flying and *CRASH*! goes the best china your mum got out in his honour.

B Your mum and dad are having a do at the Ritz to celebrate their 25th wedding anniversary. Your boyfriend is invited. On the invitation it says *Black Tie Only, Please*. He turns up wearing his best black tie, but nothing else.

C His mum and dad are having a bit of a do at the Ritz. You're up at six that morning getting ready: washing your hair, drying it, deciding you don't like it that way, washing it again, drying it again. Then more decisions: which lipstick to wear? No, not that one – it clashes with your eye liner. And is the scent he gave you for your birthday quite the way you want to smell for this particular occasion?

But at last you've got yourself ready and you arrive looking (let's not be modest) ravishing in the glitzy little number that cost you six months' pocket money.

You wonder why everyone's looking at your feet. Guess who's forgotten to change out of her trainers?

The best cure for embarrassment is not to bother with it. If you don't the chances are no one else will and, if they do, that's their business and nothing to do with you.

feelings (his)

It's his birthday. You give him the record/jumper/pet monkey he's been wanting for ages. He feels over the moon and all the happier because it was you who gave it to him. But does he show his feelings to you? You might get a "thank you", but more often it's a blank look or a grunt and you're left wondering what you've done to spoil his birthday.

It all goes back to Adam, whose first feeling was Fear of God. Fear's not a good feeling and boys have been running scared from their feelings ever since. They try to cover them up, bury them or (even better) tell themselves they haven't got any.

So what can you do? You can give him the acne treatment (i.e. leave him to sort his feelings out for himself). If he can't or won't, think twice (we're talking twice a million) before you do it for him. It's an endless job and you won't even get a "thank you" for it.

feelings (yours)

Tell him you're feeling hurt because he dropped his cricket bat on your foot (again) or forgot your birthday (again) and he'll look at you as if you're seriously sick and suggest you see a doctor. Yes, well, he would, wouldn't he? Because boys don't like having feelings (see above), they'll try to make out there's something wrong with you if you have any. Which is all the reason you need for sticking to your feelings. Try Super Stick Glue. It's the stickiest!

Flirting

Flirting is teasing and teasing is what you do to your kid brother which means that a boy who's flirting is teasing and that's what you do to your kid brother which is where we started because flirting takes you round in circles so you don't know where you are which is teasing which is flirting and if that's what he's doing . . . remember to carry a map so you can find out where you are.

Frog

When a male frog is kissed by a princess, it turns into a prince. If you're a princess, go get yourself a fishing net, catch yourself a frog, and press your lips to his.

If you're not a princesss, kissing frogs isn't recommended.

go-getter
He knows what he wants, goes for it, grabs it and gets it. If you're a go-getter yourself, watch out! When two go-getters make a grab for the cookie jar, all they're likely to get is a bump on the head.

hair
He's just been to the hairdresser's. You wish he hadn't. What do you say when he comes panting up to you, all eager, looking like a bottlebrush on legs (with the red streaks a perfect match for his bloodshot eyes and the pimple on his nose), and asks: "What do you think? Do you like it?" What do you tell him? It depends . . . If you're not that bothered if you never see him again, don't be coy. Tell him The Truth, unvarnished by consideration for his ego (all boys have one, see under *ego*) or his feelings (not all boys have them – see under *feelings*).

On the other hand, if you like everything about him except his new haircut, you have various options. You can either:

a) cross your fingers and say, "Yes, it's great" (life is a complicated business and most things have their place, white lies included);

b) be tactful and say something that could mean anything, like "Mmm"; or

c) change the subject (preferably to some other aspect of himself, e.g. how clever/strong/witty he is), in which case with a bit of luck, he'll forget the Hair question.

I
Boys' most favourite word. Hold your own and make it yours.

jokes

What a boy thinks of as a funny joke (Ha, Ha!) may not make you laugh. It may make you feel sick or nothing at all. When this happens never fake a laugh. It will only encourage him to tell another sick/unfunny joke. However, if he doesn't laugh at your jokes he has no sense of humour and you shouldn't hesitate to tell him so.

kissing

It depends on their age. Baby boys slobber kisses on anything and anyone from their teddy bear to their granny or favourite aunty. Young boys hate kissing more than washing behind their ears. But as they get older boys develop a deep interest in kissing, so watch out! They'll kiss any girl they can lay their hands on.

Some boys' kisses land on your cheek or sweetly curved mouth or wherever they're meant to. Others have no sense of direction and a kiss meant for you goes *smack*! on to the tree behind you. Maybe that's where you want it to go. And if it's not? Kissing is like playing the violin – it improves with practice. Tell him to buy himself a violin and practise on that.[1]

FOR A TREE, I'VE GOT AN INTERESTING SEX LIFE

---

1. I'm not sure I've got that right . . ..

love

If you want to know what love is, don't ask a song-writer. They're always writing about love but it's gobbledeegook. (Judge for yourself: "Love is a many-splendoured thing." Thing? Splendoured? With what and how many?)

To put it simply, love is a feeling and that's why boys try to avoid it (see *feelings*). But once smitten some boys love being in love and it's I LOVE YOU all over their T-shirts. But Freddie Lovelorn was scared witless (not that he had many wits to start with). The blood rushed to his head and his tongue got in such a twist he couldn't tell Susie Brighteyes the time, let alone "I'm all yours." Susie thought he didn't love her and couldn't eat for a whole day.[1] Learn from Susie's unhappy example.

If the boy you love has a beetroot-coloured face and not two words to say for himself, don't starve yourself. He loves you back. But if he doesn't? How can you tell? He'll tell you, or maybe drop a little hint, like a brick on your foot, to stop you running after him. It's a painful experience. To put you out of your misery, try this remedy from *The Book of Infallible Cures for Love-Sick Lovers*. I've never known it fail:

Every morning, first thing when you wake up, sit/stand in front of the mirror, look yourself in the eye and say this little rhyme:

Every day in every way
I love him less
And love me more.

You'll soon be wondering what you saw in him.

---

1. To be accurate, a quarter of a day. By break she was famished and wolfed down (ate quickly) a peanut butter sandwich.

me
The person boys put first. So should you.

macho (machismo)
A boy who's macho thinks he's got what girls want. If you want to know what the macho boy's got that he thinks girls want, you'll have to ask him because I've never been able to puzzle it out!

muscles
A boy who is proud of his muscles (lumpy, bulging shapes on arms, chest and legs) rarely has anything else to be proud of, like a brain. He longs for the return of the Cave Age, when brawn not brains was best and the brawny boy with bulging muscles was much in demand for wielding a stone club.

The stone club was the be-all and end-all of Stone Age life. It was used to protect cave-dwellers from wild animals who wanted to eat them, and to kill the wild animals *they* wanted to eat. It could be said that if it wasn't for the brawny boy and his club the human race would have died out. But now he's a sad leftover of a bygone age, hoping his time will come again. And it might. The weapons invented by brainboxes (see p.37) can blow up the world as we know it. With one big bang all mod cons will vanish, and we'll be back to the Stone Age. Be kind to the Brawny Boy. One day you may need him.

no

As recently as your grandmother's day, there was a widespread belief that a diamond was a girl's best friend. It was a belief encouraged by boys so they could treat girls as badly as they pleased and then make it up to them by popping into the jeweller's for a diamond or two. Now, however, girls who like them buy their own diamonds and they know their best friend is the word "no". It's short and its meaning is plain so that even the dimmest oaf can understand it, and delivered in the right way, it packs a hefty punch.

A girl who can say no is a girl who doesn't get what she doesn't want. It's worth practising in front of the mirror, so that when a boy you like less than your kid brother asks if he can take you home from the disco, or your kid brother asks if he can borrow your Walkman, you've got a well-aimed no for an answer.

olives

They're the fruit of a tree whose branches you wave if you've quarrelled with your boyfriend and want to make it up (see *quarrels*).

passes

You're on the school bus, minding your own business, having a peaceful chew on your after-school chewing gum. He sits beside you and its NUDGE! NUDGE! NUDGE! You think his arm has got the twitches. He thinks it's making a pass at you. You wish it wouldn't. Try the Elizabeth I treatment on the nudging arm (see *The Elizabethan Age*, p. 28). It won't nudge again.

But what if you *want* him to make a pass at you and he doesn't? Do you chance your arm and make a pass at him? It depends on how attached you are to your arm. It could be worth the risk. If you lose it, you've still got another one.

punks

Punks thrived in the 1970s and could be found in every High Street on a Saturday. They were easy to spot because they all wore the same uniform: tight jeans with holes in the knees, a T-shirt more holes than shirt, five earrings in one ear and none in the other, a safety pin through the nose and hobnailed boots. Their heads were shaved, apart from a skilfully lacquered tuft which was dyed bright pink or lime green or both.

As boy and girl punks wore the same uniform, it was difficult for the ordinary person to tell one from t'other, though doubtless they could. If there are any surviving punks, please could they write to the publishers with tips for spotting which sex is which, so that this useful information can be included in the next edition of the book.

quarrels
When you quarrel with your boyfriend you can (a) break-up or (b) make-up. (Don't try to patch it up: a patched-up quarrel is like a patched shirt – it soon needs re-mending.)

(a) Tell let's-call-him-Pete that you like let's-call-him-John better and you're going on a date (see *date*) with him. That'll break Pete up into little pieces (sometimes it's kind to be cruel) and you can dump the pieces in the recycling bin[1] on your way to the movies with John.

(b) This isn't so easy. You'll need an olive branch (see *olive*) or a white flag to wave. If you haven't either of those, which most girls haven't, you're left with saying, "Sorry". It sticks in your throat? If he's worth making up with, call a plumber to unstick it.

1. You don't want him but someone else might.

WELL, HI THERE SWEETIE!

rat

The animal variety is an unsavoury-looking creature with beady eyes, a long tail and whiskers. It lives in rubbish tips and sewers and is the first to leave a sinking ship. The male rat, by contrast, is often a strikingly handsome and deceptively charming guy, who flatters you to your face and insults you behind your back. Never give a rat a second chance. Once a rat, always a rat. Give him the boot NOW!

romance

Boys are very romantic. It's just that they don't know it. How do you let them know? Being romantic yourself doesn't work . . . suggest a walk in the moonlight and he'll think you've lost your torch. All you can do is spell it out:

W.E. A.R.E. W.A.L.K.I.N.G. I.N. T.H.E.
M.O.O.N.L.I.G.H.T. B.E.C.A.U.S.E. . . .etc.

But if he can't spell, you'll have to find a boy who can.

silly

A boy who claims he is never, ever, silly is either lying or an alien pretending to be a boy. In the case of the latter, you should immediately inform:
Fred Nutter,
Alien Detection Unit,
Crackpot House,
Downing Street,
London SW1.

supermarkets

Hundreds and thousands of people visit supermarkets every day. But you're as likely to find a boy amongst them as an iceberg in the Sahara. Although they like stuffing themselves with food, boys don't like shopping for it, cooking it or cleaning up afterwards – a characteristic they share with the pig (an animal who likes its grub but has yet to be seen, tea-towel in trotter, wiping up its trough).

If you're looking for a boy-free environment, try a supermarket.

telephone (phone)

You don't want him to phone. He's boring, a creep, the last person in the world you want to hear from. You're enjoying your favourite television programme or having a quiet night in washing your hair when *Ring! Ring!* It can't be him *again*! But it is.

Is there a law that says you have to talk to him?

"It's only polite," says your mum.

Politely tell him to boil his head in a paper bag, and replace the receiver. It's unlikely you'll find him at the other end of the line again.

OR

You want him to phone and he doesn't? Give him a ring and tell him.

um
A word used by boys who have a lot to say but can't find any other words to say it in.

vermin (see *rat*).

vulgarity
Great word, this! A word with oomph! (Say it aloud and you'll hear what I mean.) And what does it mean?

In the Dark Ages (before electric light) it meant a girl who ate her peas off the back of her knife instead of the front, or who passed wind at the table without waiting for someone to pass the wind to her.

But in our all-electric age, it doesn't mean anything. A boy who tells you otherwise is as far behind the times as your grandad, who thinks boxer shorts are trousers worn by a breed of large dog.

Wally (a type of boy)

Some boys are born Wallies. Their mums and dads look at the blob dribbling down his bib and say, "He's a born Wally." Then there are the boys who start life as Spike or Winston but as they get older people tell them, "You're a Wally". The name sticks, and they're Wally ever after.

Boys like boasting. They'll boast about the size of their biceps and how many doughnuts they can swallow in thirty seconds. (Who cares?) But you'll never hear a boy boast about being a Wally. Is this because Wallies have nothing to boast about? The question has been exercising Wally experts since the first Wally on record, Sir Wally Raleigh.

Sir Wally Raleigh was a devoted pirate in the service of Queen Elizabeth I. (see *The Elizabethan Age*, p. 28). For years he served her loyally, risking the perils of the sea to plunder Spanish ships and venturing to the New World (new to Britain but not to the Red Indians) to bring back potatoes and tobacco of which QEI was particularly fond. (There's a picture of her smoking a cigar in the National Gallery, with a Government Health Warning attached.)

Sir Wally was quite a pet of QEI until she discovered he wrote poetry. "Only Wallies write poetry. I don't want Wallies in my court! Off with his head!"

And off it came.

Wallies nowadays don't suffer such drastic treatment, but they're often cruelly mocked and their efforts to please, more often than not, come sadly unstuck. Your modern Wally stays up all night doing his homework, then leaves it on the bus so he has to stay in and do it all again. He'll half kill himself working round the clock to buy the best seats when he takes you to hear your

favourite band. You get to the concert and – surprise! surprise! – Wally's lost the tickets. Or maybe you're enjoying a quiet stroll by the river. Wally sees a dog in it. Without a thought for himself jumps in to save it. Too late he remembers dogs can swim but he can't, and you have to ruin your best coat by jumping in to save him.

Your Wally will drive you up the wall/nuts/bananas or all three at once. But think twice before you dump him. His heart is in the right place, and he'll always put you first (compare with other types of boys, p. 36).

X (ex)

How you feel about your ex-boyfriend depends on how you parted. Did he jump or was he pushed? If you gave him the push you may still want him for a friend. If he jumped hand-in-hand with the girl you thought was your best mate, you're more likely to want his head

served up on a plate with an apple in his mouth. This was the fate of John the Baptist when he spurned Salome. John the Baptist was later made into a saint. Unless you want your ex to be canonized, keep a cool head, let him keep his, and write him off as a nasty experience.

yawn
A wide opening of the mouth left uncovered by boys who are under the illusion you want to look at their tonsils (see *yob*, p. 36).

zits
Girls have them, boys don't (see *acne*, p. 47).